Praise for
FATHERS, BROTHERS, AND SONS

"Frank has been a close friend for thirty-five years. From dealing with being abandoned by his father, to the tragedy of his brother's murder, to the rise of Anthrax, it's all here in Frankie's unmistakable, sincere, and at times humorous voice. I am so proud of him for telling his long overdue life story in such a candid and honest way."

—Eddie Trunk, SiriusXM Radio

"What's great and memorable about *Fathers, Brothers, And Sons* is the complete honesty that comes off the pages... As you read them, it feels like Frank is sitting next to you at a bar."   —Knac.com

"I could not put this book down. Frank is an amazing storyteller."

—*The Aquarian*

"I can honestly say Frank's life story reads as though you're having a direct conversation with him."   —*Rewind It*

"A fascinating and open story."   —*Houston Press*

"The underlying message in this book is resiliency and meeting challenges head-on. Frank's life and successful career in Anthrax since 1984 is proof of that."   —*Sonic Perspectives*

"Frank speaks candidly and with utter honesty."   —*UnRated*

"Entertaining, thought-provoking reading."   —Goodreads

"Bello's storytelling reveals a man willing to connect with a heavy metal audience in a unique way."   *Outburn*

"Frank is usually the guy with the biggest smile on his face at an Anthrax concert, so this book may surprise people with some of the life events he's endured over the years." —*V13*

"Although it deals with some delicate and tragic circumstances, it never descends into pitying melodrama." —*The Razor's Edge*

"A bold and heartening autobiography." —*Record Collector*

"*Fathers, Brothers, And Sons* doesn't dish all the usual tell-all dirt... His memoir instead embraces the positive within the darkness." —*Billboard*

"Cool stories from a guy who loves his family and loves music. That's what life is all about. Thank you, Frank, for inspiring us all." —Steven A McKay, author

"Very readable and engaging. Well worth your time." —*Metal Rules*

"You'll love it." —Corey Taylor, Slipknot

FATHERS, BROTHERS, AND SONS

FATHERS, BROTHERS, AND SONS
SURVIVING ANGUISH, ABANDONMENT, AND ANTHRAX
FRANK BELLO

WITH JOEL McIVER

RARE BIRD

Los Angeles, Calif.

THIS IS A GENUINE RARE BIRD BOOK

Rare Bird Books
6044 North Figueroa Street
Los Angeles, CA 90042
rarebirdbooks.com

FIRST NORTH AMERICAN PAPERBACK EDITION

Set in Dante
Printed in the United States

PAPERBACK ISBN: 9781644283028

10 9 8 7 6 5 4 3 2 1

Publisher's Cataloging-in-Publication data

Names: Bello, Frank, author. | McIver, Joel, author.
Title: Fathers, brothers, and sons: surviving anguish, abandonment, and Anthrax
/ Frank Bello; with Joel McIver.
Description: Includes index. | First Paperback Edition | A Genuine Rare Bird
Book | New York, NY; Los Angeles, CA: Rare Bird Books, 2023.
Identifiers: ISBN 9781644282311 (hardcover) | 978-1-64428-302-8 (paperback) |
978-1-64428-248-9 (ebook) | Subjects: LCSH Bello, Frank. | Anthrax (Musical
group: U.S.) | Rock musicians—United States—Biography. | Heavy metal music.
| Rock music. | BISAC BIOGRAPHY & AUTOBIOGRAPHY /
Music | MUSIC / Genres & Styles / Heavy Metal

Classification: LCC ML420.B45 B45 2021 | DDC 782.42166/092—dc23

THIS BOOK IS DEDICATED to the strong women in my life who raised me and instilled the strength in me to always strive to be a better man—my mother, Rose, my grandmother, Tina, and my wife, Teresa.

I also dedicate this book to my son, Brandon. This is how your dad did it, and you can do it, too. Never say die, and never say "I should have."

Finally, this book is dedicated to my brother, Anthony, who was taken from us in 1996. You were the best of us. We will meet again.

Contents

7 Foreword *by Gene Simmons*

11 Preface *2023*

13 Introduction

15 Chapter 1 *Ass-Kickings and Eggplants*

27 Chapter 2 *First Kiss*

40 Chapter 3 *Into the Madhouse*

53 Chapter 4 *Armed and Diseased*

66 Chapter 5 *Island Life*

78 Chapter 6 *Cliff*

89 Chapter 7 *Who's the Man?*

100 Chapter 8 *Euphoric Persistence*

111 Chapter 9 *Acting Up*

126 Chapter 10 *Anthony*

141 Chapter 11 *Cathartic Days*

154 Chapter 12 *Helmets On*

166 Chapter 13 *Brandon*

175 Chapter 14 *Buckling Up*

191 Chapter 15 *Father, Brother, Son*

205 Acknowledgments

207 Index

Foreword
by Gene Simmons

B EING MEN, WE TEND not to talk about our emotions. If you say, "Hi, how are you?" to a woman, she'll immediately tell you her life story, but we don't share our emotions—even though we all have deep wounds in us.

It's shameful how fathers, the male of the species, tend not to stick around for their families. It's not always because they have problems with alcohol and drugs. Sometimes men just give up and walk out on their kids. When you do that, you don't realize that you have scarred forever a young child who thinks they did something wrong.

"What did I do wrong that my father left me?"

That's a question you'll never be able to answer. I never have. My father left us when I was about seven years old, and even though I bought him houses and supported him until the day he died, I never went to visit him, and I did not go to his funeral. Of course, after that happened, I was ashamed. Like I said, those wounds will never heal. They last for a lifetime.

Thank God for this thing that we do: this suit of armor we wear onstage. Like Gestalt therapy, or Dr. Janov's primal scream therapy— look it up!—playing music allows us to be in a padded room and scream our heads off to try and get the rage out. It's part and parcel of what Frank's band Anthrax and my band Kiss does. We get up and play aggressive music, and it's an outlet. It lets out some of that rage, at least for a while. When you're quiet for a while, it creeps back, so it's good to keep playing onstage in front of people.

In this book, Frank talks about finding healing by being a loving father himself. This was also the case for me. I was hesitant to get married forever. I met the loveliest woman, Shannon, and we were together for twenty-nine years before we got married. We had two kids together, and still I refused to get married—until I finally married her when I was the age of sixty-two. We've been married for nine years now, and it's getting better and better—but I was always afraid when I confronted myself.

I was afraid that I would turn into my father and abandon the family.

I have not done so.

In this book, you'll read Frank's memories of hanging around outside our management office in New York back in the seventies, waiting for Kiss to come out so he and his pal Tom could talk to us. I remember all those times, and I have to tell you, those memories stand out for me just as much as my memories of playing in front of 50,000 or 100,000 people. That's terrific, too, but on a completely different level, because there's no intimacy. You don't get to have a conversation with somebody in that situation.

On the other hand, when you see the wide-eyed sense of wonder of a fan who comes up to you, you see what it's really about. Above the fame, above the money, above the women, above all that, is the connection being made by band and fan—and we got it back, don't kid yourself. If you think fans like Frank and his pal Tom got off on us, the fact that they had that bright-eyed sense of wonder got us off in return. It made us think, "This is what it's really about."

I remember when I was a fan myself. I used to hang out and bug Stan Lee and his secretary Flo Steinberg at the Marvel Comics office, and Stan used to write me postcards saying, "You will do great things. Hang in there, true believer," and all that stuff. It was like a message from the gods to me as a little kid.

I think the great ones never forget where they came from. What Frank and his pal did was reignite the fire in us, as a reminder that we got everything we wanted. When they came around to talk to us, Frank thought he was bugging us—but it's actually the opposite. I hope he'll tell you that when he came around to bug us, we actually had conversations. Truth be told, it meant a lot to us.

All these years later, Frank has fans of his own. For those of you out there who want to hear something fresh, put on your Anthrax records and turn the bass up, along with some high end so you can hear the actual notes that Frank plays. You'll hear some very interesting stuff. As in a string quartet, he does what the cello would do. That idea goes back to the baroque era and the Renaissance, and to The Beatles. When you heard Paul McCartney's bass lines, they were hooks in and of themselves, and they didn't just follow the drums. Sometimes they jumped off the drums and went against them, or dropped out altogether. Train your ears and listen to what Frank's bass is doing.

This is the important thing. When a little wide-eyed kid who wants to play bass comes up to Frank, I'm sure that Frank won't forget himself as a little wide-eyed kid, too. I hope he takes the time to inspire that young fan—because in a very real way, life is about a relay race. You run the best race you can, and then right in front of you is someone who hasn't run the race yet. Pass the baton on as fast and as well as you can and let them run their own race.

Gene Simmons, 2021

Preface
2023

WELCOME TO THE NEW edition of my autobiography! Whether you bought it, borrowed it, or stole it, you're reading it—which is what's most important.

The first hardback edition of *Fathers, Brothers, and Sons* was published by Rare Bird in November 2021. I'm writing this new preface for the paperback edition a year later—and it feels like the world has gotten even crazier in that short time. Covid is still around, there's a war in Ukraine, there's a global recession on the way, and there's headlines every single day about something terrible happening.

My book doesn't try to solve those problems, but it does offer help to anyone who has been through the things I've been through. The biggest thing for me has been the feedback I've gotten from people, which has overwhelmed me. What people are telling me is that this book has helped them, which means more than anything. That's what I wanted the book to do. If I could help one person with my book, that meant its job was done, and I think we've done that.

I get emails, texts, and social media comments all the time. People are even telling me that the book has helped their relationships with their fathers, and I didn't even have a father, so you can imagine how incredible it is to hear that. That's strong stuff, and I didn't expect that at all. These people are finding closure, and that's bigger than any book or any rock band.

Sometimes I have to read messages like these two or three times just so they can sink in, because they aren't just words. People get the emotion that I felt when I was writing the book, and they also like the audiobook for that reason—maybe because there was emotion in the way that I read it.

I was petrified when the book came out, I admit. I've never been that honest or open about my personal life before. Only my family knows what I went through, and only my therapist knew how painful and scary that stuff was. Putting all that in print, and holding nothing back so it was a cleansing process for me, was terrifying. I had to let it all out, and I think people totally understood that.

As I mentioned in the introduction below, my cowriter, Joel, and I donated a chunk of our revenue from this book to two charities: For The Children (forthechildren.org) and National Fatherhood Initiative (fatherhood.org). Thank you for investing your hard-earned cash in this new edition, as well as your time. In this day and age, I don't take any of that for granted.

Stay healthy, take care of your families, and I'll see you on the road.

Frank Bello

New York, November 2022

Introduction

WELCOME TO THIS BOOK! We're going to have a lot of fun together, believe me, but we're going to talk about some serious stuff, too. I'm a happy guy and I like to think I'm a funny one, too—don't we all?—but there's an angry man inside me, too.

I don't like that guy.

Say I'm driving somewhere with my wife, Teresa, and some idiot cuts me off. I'll be instantly fucking raging and ready to kill that guy, and I'll start exhibiting all the signs of road rage. That's when Teresa will say "Frank!" in that "wife tone." All wives have that 'wife tone,' and thank God they do. I used to fight it, and answer, "What?" but now I go, "You're right," because it makes no sense to get that angry. Where's it going to get you? In trouble.

That angry guy has been there all my life. My therapists tell me that abandonment by my father when I was a kid is a big part of it. You might have been through some of that stuff yourself, and if so, the idea behind this book is to offer you ways to deal with the emotions caused by all that, like the rage I just talked about. You saw what Gene wrote in his foreword. He's been through all this shit, too.

Why did I write this book now? Well, you get to a certain age and you start to reflect. Now that I'm in my fifties, I've come to realize what a great ride my life has been. I'm not done yet, though, and I don't want to deal with the angry guy inside me for the rest of my life. Enough is enough, and I don't want my son, Brandon, to suffer any negative consequences from it. That's the most important thing in my life—to be a great dad to Brandon, and to heal the anger that I feel. And you know what? Being a good dad is how I deal with it. I think a lot of men, young and old, could learn from that.

As this book took shape in 2020 and 2021, and it became obvious that it was going to address some serious subjects, my cowriter Joel and I decided to donate a portion of the proceeds to relevant charities. There are a ton of great, courageous organizations out there battling to raise awareness of the damage done when parents abandon their families, but these two particularly appealed to us:

For The Children, www.forthechildren.org
National Fatherhood Initiative, www.fatherhood.org

Thanks for buying this book. In doing so, you're helping out a whole lot of people who urgently need it.

I want this book to be a comfortable conversation between us—just a chat between friends, maybe over a coffee or a beer. Think of it that way. We're just fans of music, so let's just talk about it and see where we end up.

Now let's get started. Man, have I got some crazy stuff to tell you...

1
Ass-Kickings and Eggplants

A S MY FRIEND DIMEBAG used to say… "Let's go!"

I was born on July 9, 1965, in the Bronx in New York. My mother, Rose, is a strong woman. She had to be—she had five kids. I was the oldest, and then my siblings Suzanne, Tonianne, Charles, and Anthony followed. Even with so many of us, Mom was always there for me, any time I needed her. God bless her.

My dad was an oil-burner mechanic, and his job was to go to different places and fix them. Now I look back at that time of my life, I know that he had a good heart and that he was very generous, because whatever he had, he would give it to you. At the same time, I'm pretty sure I have a hot temper thanks to the things I witnessed when I was young.

Where his anger came from I don't know, but even when I was young, I knew that was how I didn't want to be. To this day, if people tell me I have a temper, it hits home because I don't want to be like him.

We had a nice, three-bedroom house, of around 1,500 square feet, in a beautiful neighborhood in Rockland County where there was a good school system. That sounds great, right? Well, it was, but it all changed when I was around ten years old, because my dad left.

Even before he left, I knew things weren't right between him and my mom. I clearly remember the pain of watching them fight. I don't even want to think about some of the arguments that they had. It was really ugly, and it remains embedded in my brain more than forty-five years later. Like Gene said in his foreword, some wounds never heal; well, he's right about that.

My poor mom was left with no money, which makes me really angry, even now. She didn't work because she was a housewife looking after a big family. Back in the day, a woman was the wife and looked after the kids, and the man went out and was the breadwinner. But he left her with nothing, so what could she do? I remember her calling his office and everybody there covering for him, saying, "Oh, he hasn't been here today." But my mom knew the truth, and that broke my heart. I knew it, too. I didn't want to think it, but I knew.

We continued to live in the old house for a little while, but repossession notices were starting to come in because we had no income and the mortgage wasn't being paid. There was very little food and I remember one time seeing my mom, standing at the stove, crying. This memory fucks me up to this day. She was making Rice-A-Roni as a meal. It was the last food in the house, and she was worried that there wasn't going to be enough for all five kids. Of course, it was never going to be enough for all of us.

I can talk about this now because I've had therapy and I want people to understand, but it still hurts. What I can't understand, and I've asked my dad this question and he didn't have an answer for me, was how you can leave a family of five with no money, especially when one of them—my brother Anthony—was still a baby. How does any human being leave a family like that? I have no answer to that question, either, because I can't imagine ever doing it myself.

My mom was strong, though, and she kept us together, even through her own horrible pain. She got a job, and she got a driver's license so she could drive us around. Thank God for her strength.

When we lost the house, we moved to a low-income apartment in Haverstraw, which was not the best of neighborhoods. I went to a public school there, and as if the family being abandoned with no money and having to move out of our nice house wasn't enough, now my problems got even worse—because I got beat up every day on the way to school.

I mean this literally. Every single day, I got my ass kicked by bigger guys than me. I don't know why; I guess there were some neighborhood bullies who enjoyed beating up kids smaller than them.

I remember there was one specific guy that got me every day, with his buddy to help him. I had to take this one path to school, and this dude waited on that path with his friend. He'd look for ways to start with me. I'd try to keep walking past him, but he'd come right up in front of me and stop me, so I couldn't get away, and then he'd start punching me.

I don't know why he didn't like me. I didn't exactly have time to ask him; he was too busy hitting me. This motherfucker was huge, and I was just a little kid, so I had no chance.

I remember this clearly because it scarred me mentally; I later went to therapy for this. I could only get away from his abuse by hiding under nearby cars. I'm not kidding. I'd stay under the fucking car until he would leave, and then I would go to school.

I remember this prick's name to this day, and while we were writing this book, my cowriter Joel found him on Facebook. I haven't looked him up myself, though, and obviously I'm not going to name him here. Anyway, I always say the bullying built character, just to laugh about it. Laughter is a big deal in my life;

people say I'm a funny guy, and I'm glad to hear that, but ask any comedian in the world where their comedy comes from, and they'll tell you it comes from a lot of pain.

Joking aside, the bullying I received from this kid was genuinely terrible, and if I even smell bullying these days, I deal with it very quickly. I'm no tough guy, but I'm the prick that you really don't want to deal with in that situation. With all the therapy I've been through, my anger at being bullied is still there, although I suppress it. Like I said, that anger is never leaving me. I don't like it because it's a constant battle.

So here I was, getting beat up every single day. I couldn't believe this bullshit. My life had been going good, and then we lost the house, and now I'm getting my ass kicked. I thought, "What the fuck is going on?"

After a few months of this, I was starting to wonder how my mental health would get through it, let alone the physical side. The daily beatings were getting worse; these were really violent attacks, and I couldn't do anything about it. I even learned karate, and tried out all those moves, but you can't win a fight when there are two guys, both bigger than you, beating you up.

Mentally, I wasn't the same person anymore because the insecurity was building up in me, which turned into anger. I was so angry about being insecure. I knew I was either going to die or run away.

There was only one solution in that situation. I had to move out and go to a different school, so when I was eleven, I moved in with my grandmother in the Bronx. I left my mom with the four younger kids, which was a great source of guilt to me because I was her oldest son, even though I did it out of necessity.

Fortunately, my mom thought it was the obvious thing to do; she could see that I was freaking the fuck out. I honestly felt that

I had to move away from Haverstraw to survive. I give my mother a lot of credit for that, because that was a hard choice, to let your son live with someone else.

•••

MY GRANDMOTHER WAS BERNADETTE Benante, although we all called her Tina. Her house at Graff Avenue in the Bronx immediately felt like home. Actually, it had always felt like home: I remember going over to Tina's house because it was always such a warm, welcoming place. It really meant a lot to me. It was, no pun intended, my safe home because it was where I always felt secure. When I moved in, I felt as if a huge weight had lifted from me.

Tina's son Charlie Benante was my uncle, although he was only three years older than me; Tina had had him relatively late in life. Charlie had four sisters, the oldest being my mom, Rose. The others were my aunt Angela, my aunt Susan, and my aunt Laurie; the only one who lived there when I lived there was Laurie. She was closer to my age, so she was more like a big sister to me than an aunt.

Charlie's dad, my grandfather Charles, was full Italian, and he passed in 1966, when Charlie was four years old. I always felt bad for Charlie because he lost his father when he was so young. I remember sitting on my grandfather's lap at the kitchen table and playing games with him while he sang to me. I love that memory. I wish I had more time with him because I think I could have learned a lot from him about life as my father was no use to me.

Charlie was like a big brother to me. I'm very grateful to him for letting me come and live in his house when we were kids and including me as an everyday family member. That's not easy to do, but we were always close, maybe because we were so similar in age.

This was a very loving environment. Tina should have been Saint Tina—I hold her in that much regard. She was the best person on Earth. I have great memories of her talking to me about the right and wrong things in life. Whatever you believe spiritually, I believe that my grandmother was put on Earth to be an angel to me and my family. I still feel like that today.

The three most important women in my life have been my wife, Teresa, my mother, Rose, and my grandmother, Tina. My aunt Laurie was also a big part of my life, as was her sister Susan. I have great love for all of these women who shaped me to be the man I am. They were always there for me.

I believe that strong women are not appreciated enough in our society. I would love to see a female president. I really would because we would all benefit. In America it's so male-driven; everybody likes to fight. We men think we have to be dominant and masculine, and I hate that. That's why so many people in this world are the way they are.

Women have a better sense of what people are. There's something about that perspective that I really appreciate. It's nurturing, regardless of whether they're hard women or soft women. I love them all because they have something somewhere in their hearts that makes them care.

Talking of nurturing, let me talk a minute about the food my grandmother made. To this day, I'm a sucker for great food. I was very lucky to grow up in a house with the best cook in the world. I remember getting ready for the great family meals we had every Sunday, hoping Tina would make the peppers and eggs, or the gravy with sausages and meatballs, or ravioli, or eggplant parmegiana.

Oh, my God, the eggplant parmegiana! She used to do it the right way, where she used to skin the eggplant. Some people are allergic to that skin, and it makes their lips itch if they eat it.

I'm one of those, and I love eggplant, so whenever I eat it in a restaurant, I'm scratching my lips all the time. When I ate it at my grandmother's, though, it was never like that.

She cooked the best of the best, and it was always made with love. Imagine the typical Italian grandmother—that's who Tina was. She cared about everything.

It was my saving grace for life, that house, that block, that neighborhood, those people. Things would have gone a different way for me if I didn't have that security and support, because the people in the neighborhood were so great. I was friends with all the kids who lived nearby.

My new school was great, too. It was PS 72, and I was at that school for fifth grade. On my first day, I was still very insecure, affected by what I'd been through. I didn't know if there would be bullies at this school, too, but thankfully I met a bunch of good people and things really took off from there.

I did get jumped once when I was in sixth or seventh grade. By then I was at IS 192 in the Bronx, or Piagentini-Jones Intermediate School, to give it its full name. That was a horrible day. I was going to school like I did every day, taking the local MTA bus and getting off outside my school. I don't know why, but three kids attacked me. One kid jumped on my back while another was swinging at me, and the third one was kicking me from the side. I still remember that the kid on my back held back my arms, and while he was doing that, he actually started to bite my back. I could feel the cut on my back from the biting.

So all three of them were really giving me a beating. Thankfully I was good at taking care of myself, so I flipped the first guy off my back. I know it sounds like a fight in a movie, but I swear this is true, and then I ran into the school. I limped to the principal's office and told them I got jumped.

It became this big thing because the principal sent me home. My aunt Laurie saw me and freaked out, went to the school, and made a huge stink about it. You see what I mean about being a strong woman? She got the job done when usually you would have gone to your dad to get it taken care of. Laurie took charge because there was no dad.

The absence of a father is why, while I'm alive, I will never let my son be without. Never. I probably spoil him too much, as fathers like me do, but I'm in every nook and cranny of his life because I was raised by strong women, and that's the truth.

This is a short life that we have, and if I can help anybody that went through anything similar to what I did, that's my goal. There's so much in a word that can help you get through to the next day. I knew about depression, and being scared, and being insecure in school growing up, and getting my ass kicked because I didn't have the backbone from a father who should have taught me to have one. I want you, the reader, to know that it's possible to survive this. If you have a strong parent, or someone supportive in your life, and hopefully you have at least one of those, you can do it. That's the truth.

Abandonment is a big deal to me. There's so much of that around today. Whatever kind of person you are, abandonment has everything to do with how you grow as a person. I thank God for my family. Without them, I think I would have been in jail or dead.

Back to the Bronx. Here I was, living in a safe home, enjoying a pretty normal life, except for rare incidents like the one I just mentioned. I was a sports guy outside of school and played a lot of baseball. My uncle Joe, who was married to my aunt Sue, ran a deli on Harding Avenue and, around 1980 when I was fifteen, gave me a job there for two dollars an hour. It was around the block from my grandmother's house, so I used to walk there after school and work there from 3:30 p.m. to 8:00 p.m.

So now I was a deli guy, a cashier, and I used to cut meat. I was still working at Joe's Deli when Anthrax's first record came out four years later. I would come off a tour, where we got five dollars a day per diem, and go right back into the deli to make money to live. I'm still an amazing meat-cutter to this day. I can make a sandwich like nobody. I totally enjoyed it because I'm a people person and I got to know the customers. The store was in a good area, but there were some scary times. Joe got robbed a couple of times at gunpoint, but luckily for me, I wasn't there when that happened.

My uncle Joe has always been a father figure to me. He really took me under his wing and I learned a lot of life lessons from him. He taught me the rights and wrongs, because once again, I had no direction from any other man. This time was definitely my growing up as a man. I learned a lot at that deli.

Uncle Joe was only about ten years older than me, so I could relate to him easily. Of course, I had lots of strong women in my life, but it was important to have a man to look up to. Any fatherly advice I had when I was young came from Joe.

Joe couldn't understand how any guy could leave his kids, because he's a good father who takes care of his loved ones. He saw what we went through when my mother was left alone with five kids and I moved over to my grandmother's house, and he cared deeply about us.

He and my aunt Sue would ask me, because they were always concerned about my future, "Where are you putting the money you're making in the deli?" Not that it was a lot of money, but it was the only money I had, so I would give them whatever cash I didn't need for records and whatever, and they would keep it in an envelope for me, because I didn't have a bank account.

Joe really showed me the importance of saving a dollar. I can't credit him enough for how much I learned at his store. I remember

Joe showing me the right way to work the cash register and to give the right change, because you need to be able to count money correctly in this life. He'd show me how to use the meat-cutter safely, too, putting the guard on so I didn't injure myself.

Other little things I learned were important too: for example, I'd be stocking shelves, so I'd walk over to a box of food cans, label one, and then walk back to the shelf and put the can on it. Joe would say, "Take the box over to the shelf and save yourself a trip each time."

These lessons teach you how to make things easier for yourself—and those lessons have served me well throughout my life. Life is going to be hard work whatever you do, so let's learn ways to make it easier for ourselves.

Joe gave me some good advice about relationships, too. When I talked to him about a girl who came into the deli that I wanted to date, he'd say, "Be careful with that one," and, "Make sure you put a rubber on your hammer!" This wasn't just work advice—these were serious life lessons for a teenager.

When I wasn't working, there was nothing better than hanging out with my family in my grandmother's house, or with my friends from the neighborhood, just having dinner on a Sunday afternoon, or at birthday parties. Man, I remember some great times. Our neighbors would come over and play cards with my aunts in the evenings. They used to call me a *yenta*, which is a Yiddish word meaning "gossip," because I'd sit in the corner and listen to all their life stories. They'd talk about who they hated, and who this one bastard was, and who this other schmuck was, and all this great gossip, and they'd be drinking tons of coffee and smoking up a storm.

There was never any harm in all this gossip, though, and I loved to listen to it, because they were true life stories. I'd think, "Wow—

that happens?" and take it in, like a fly on the wall. I remember one guy had serious flatulence, which was hilarious to me. At any given time, the women would suddenly scream, "Did you fart?" I loved it. Those were great days.

And at Christmas? Damn, I wish I could take you there right now, just for the food alone. It was like a Martin Scorsese film but in real life.

On Christmas Eve, everybody came to my grandmother's house, all parts of the family, because she was the matriarch. She was the love of the family; she kept everybody together through love, not discipline. You just wanted to be around her.

Everybody—my mother, the in-laws, people's boyfriends and girlfriends, the neighbors—everybody was there. The atmosphere, full of love, was a draw for them, and the food was another one, a big one. There was everything, from the breaded shrimp she made, to the three-colored cookies she baked because she was the best baker in the world. If you've never heard of three-colored Italian cookies, find them on the internet immediately. Even so, the pictures you see are nowhere near what my grandma could do. Days before Christmas, she'd start preparing them.

Everything was made from scratch; she'd be cooking nonstop for that one Christmas Eve. I'm telling you, she went from soup to nuts, from the snacks and the appetizers to the main meals and fish and pasta and meat, whatever anybody wanted, and cheesecakes and pies. Of course, everybody brought their own food over as well, and the wine was flowing. I'm telling you, it's a miracle I didn't weigh 500 pounds when I was living there.

And then imagine the presents. Nobody was rich, because we were all very blue-collar people, but everybody made a decent living, so we would all get gifts. We'd wait until midnight before opening the presents, apart from my mother, who couldn't wait that long and would start ripping them open at 11:30 p.m. That was even more fun. And then you ended the night with coffee and pastries and cake, so you didn't get out of there until two or three in the morning. You'd come down on Christmas Day and you'd almost feel like you had a hangover without having drunk any booze. You'd practically be in a food coma! But you'd feel so fucking satisfied, not just because of the food, but because of the love and the energy and the vibe in that house, which had such a glow on it.

All this is God's honest truth, spoken from my heart. I miss those days, because as you get older, families fragment and different segments have their own children. We all love each other, and we all see each other occasionally, but it's nowhere like those old days.

I feel like the luckiest person on Earth to have had those days, coming from where I came from. Those people were always so supportive to me, my siblings, and my mom because they knew what we'd been through. That's what great families do.

2
First Kiss

L OOKING BACK AT THIS time, which I guess is around 1980 to late 1983, before I joined Anthrax, I know that there were two paths I could have taken in life.

As I said, I spent all my time working at my uncle Joe's deli, and on Friday nights, a group of young Italian kids that I affectionately call "guidos" would come in to say hi. I was friendly with them. They were good guys and I didn't see any harm in them. Just like the Italian guys in *Saturday Night Fever*, they got paid on a Friday night, so they wanted to go drinking at the clubs and blow all their dough. They'd come home the next day, either hungover or still drunk, totally broke with nothing to show for their week's work.

They invited me to go out to the club every Friday, and I remember this one Friday night in early 1981. These guys burst through the door, all excited because it was the end of the week, and they were going out to get fucked up.

"Hey, Frankie!"

"Frankie, come on! Get your shit together!"

"Come on, man, we're going out. Let's go!"

I laughed and said no.

I know what you're thinking. It's the early eighties, the coolest time in the whole of history to go out on the town in old-school,

Martin Scorsese-style New York—and I said no? What idiot would turn down that opportunity?

Well, it so happens that I had a solid reason not to go out and get wasted that night. It was February 21, 1981, and on that day, Rush was releasing their new album, *Moving Pictures*. It's almost impossible for me to overstate the importance of rock music to me now, let alone how essential it was to me back then. Bands like Rush were like gods to me.

This is why I didn't go out that night. I knew that *Moving Pictures* was coming out the following day, so I wasn't about to go out with those guys, because early the next morning I was going to a store called Records & Stuff on Westchester Square to stand in line to get it. I planned to buy it with the money that I earned at the deli. That's where my money was going—I'd saved up for that record instead of spending it on partying. I thought that Rush album was much more important than getting loaded, and looking back on how my career started, I was dead right.

By the way, I don't have anything against getting loaded. As you'll see in later chapters, I have been well and truly fucked up more times than I care to remember, although that came later. Back in the deli days, though, I didn't really drink much. Even when my friends were partying and I went to hang out with them, I was a half-beer guy, maybe because I wasn't brought up into heavy drinking. I was more into food. Any restaurant you wanted to go to, no problem—I was there.

I didn't do drugs either, while we're on the subject of getting loaded. There was this one time, when I was maybe fourteen, when I was with a friend and he brought out some speed. I inhaled that shit right after him, just so I'd look cool, and I had the worst fucking reaction in the world. It felt like my eyes were going to blow up. I had this extreme pain in my sinuses, and my nose started running heavily. I started choking, and I thought, "What the fuck is happening?"

I don't know if it was an allergic reaction or what, but whatever it was, that incident made me swear off drugs from that point on. Drugs were just not me. That was the right choice, of course. A lot of my friends went another way over the years—and look, whatever people choose to do, it's their life and their decision—but I'm glad I didn't go that way myself. To this day, people will say to me, "Hey, Frank, want a bump?" and I always think, "Why would I want to put that stuff in my nose?"

I love the smell of pot, on the other hand, because it's a sense memory that reminds me of seeing cool gigs. I don't smoke it, though, because it fucks up my throat and I can't sing. I tried it once and it burned my throat. Another good lesson. It just never took, and I'm glad it didn't take.

I didn't smoke cigarettes either, because my grandfather on my father's side used to smoke Parliaments. He and my grandmother on that side, my Nanny, had been born in Italy and emigrated to America, and I remember Pop Pop, as I called him in the Italian way, sitting with his jug of wine on the deck of the house, watching life go by. He'd have a pack of Parliaments right there, and he'd be inhaling every one. Pop Pop smoked multiple packs a day, and what I don't forget, and what turned me off smoking permanently, was the sound of the cough he had. The depth of that sound was scary.

I knew, even then, that smoking was the reason for that cough, and God rest his soul, he passed of emphysema. What's strange is that the smell of his cigarettes was fucking great for some reason. It made me feel at home and comfortable and safe.

Pop Pop was the first person who turned me on to wine, because—as the Italians used to do back then—they make you try it when you're a kid, because it's supposed to be good for your health. He also made homemade wine, and it was nothing like the usual homemade crap. It was amazing.

Pop Pop lived a different way of life, and I understood that, and I loved that about the old school. A lot of those older people lived a good, long, happy, healthy life, and I think part of that was due to the wine they drank. I was close to Nanny and Pop Pop until my parents split.

We've talked about booze and drugs, so we might as well talk about sex. I was a horny fuck from the age of twelve, always spanking and cranking with the best of them over a copy of *Playboy* magazine. When it came to actually having sex, though, that was late by today's standards—I was around seventeen. I didn't have too many girlfriends before that, just girls I really liked.

The problem was this: I knew, from the very beginning, that I couldn't have anyone or anything stand in the way of my love of music. It was Charlie who got me into music, and I thank him from the bottom of my heart for that. Without him, I might still have become a musician, but I would have been a half-assed one. I saw how dedicated he was, and I love him to this day for being such a dedicated musician that he inspired me to do the same myself.

Charlie had started playing drums at an incredibly young age, and I'd watch him play and think, "If Charlie can do this, I can do this, too." Seeing this, he encouraged me to do it, so I started playing guitar in 1977 or '78, when I was twelve or thirteen.

As I learned to play, I also learned to love music. Rush was one of my first loves, but not the very first, as we'll see. My obsession with them was total, so if I had to keep going back to a Rush record to learn what Geddy Lee was playing, and a girl was calling me to hang out, guess who was going to win? You got it. Music was my first love.

In the case of *Moving Pictures*, released that weekend in February 1981, I'd just started playing bass as well as guitar, and that album turned out to be my training on bass, so it was the right decision. That's where my drive was, and thankfully something told me instinctually that this was a better route than going out to try and get laid and party.

Rock stars seemed so untouchable back then. You could never dream of meeting them. The only famous person I ever met when I was a kid was Chubby Checker, whom I saw in 1976 on East Tremont Avenue in the Bronx. He was going into a candy store, and we were in the car outside, double-parked. My aunt said, "That's Chubby Checker!" and we all went, "Hey, Chubby!" so he said hi. It was so surreal because his big hit "The Twist" was still huge back then.

Now, imagine the thought of meeting Rush back then. You couldn't even form that thought in your mind, because as I said, they were like gods. And yet there was another band in my life who were even more important than Rush. To this day, I can't explain how big they were to me.

•••

THE FIRST KISS ALBUM I ever heard was *Alive!*

Charlie had it, and as soon as I saw it, it was all over for me. I was immediately in love. I was all wide-eyed like, "What is this? It looks great!" I clearly remember opening up that record, seeing the artwork, and putting it on the turntable, with the crackle of vinyl and then the crowd shouting, "Kiss! Kiss! Kiss!"

I was like, "What the fuck is going on?"

If you closed your eyes, it was like being at the show, and all of a sudden these great songs came on. Kiss hit home as soon as I heard them. They connected with me at a primal, gut level.

This was my thing now. That was it. Nothing else mattered. Kiss were my new heroes—right then and there. It was superhero time, and my superheroes played great music.

I hadn't seen them live or on TV, and of course there was no internet, so I'd have to imagine the band playing while I listened to the songs. I didn't know who was singing—whether it was Paul or Gene, or what—or who was playing which instrument. I had a vision in my head of the four faces, and I would think, "Who's doing what? Is it Gene the Demon, Paul the Starchild, Ace the Spaceman, or Peter the Cat?" And then when I finally saw them on TV, I was like, "Oh, my God!" It was all over for me then, even more so.

Now, when I first saw Kiss it was at Nassau Coliseum in New York on February 21, 1977, on the Rock and Roll Over Tour. It was my first show, at the age of eleven. I went with Charlie and my friend Tom. They played some songs from the new record *Love Gun*, which came out later that year. Sammy Hagar was supporting, but we got there too late to see him.

Let me tell you something about that show. Kiss were as big in 1977 as whoever the biggest pop artist is now. I have no idea who that is, but whoever it is, Kiss were as big, or bigger. The atmosphere was electric. This was back in the raw rock 'n' roll days, and they were great times.

There was a definite vibe, starting in the parking lot, where everybody was partying with their Kiss signs and whatnot. People were smoking pot everywhere, and that smell of weed was so delicious, even though we didn't smoke it ourselves. And the girls were so beautiful, oh, my God. Everything was happening at once.

Everybody was there for one reason, and there was so much energy and no negativity at all. We were asking each other, "What's their set list going to be like?" "Is Paul going to have that blond streak on the side of his hair?" "What's Gene going to be like?" "Is Peter going to put some green makeup on his face?"

This is how crazy we were about Kiss—we even knew that sometimes Peter Criss would use green makeup, and sometimes he wouldn't. These are the tiny details that you think about when you're that crazy about something. You didn't know the answers, and that was part of the excitement. You had no idea what the set list was going to be—and then we went into the show itself...

Oh, my fucking God. Let me tell you right now: the opening of a Kiss show in the seventies was like the opening of no show by any other band, *ever*. You didn't know exactly how they were going to fuck you up, but you knew it was going to happen somehow, because there were going to be some pyro explosions, the staging was going to be incredible, and it was going to be insanely theatrical. In effect, you were going to the theater with your friends that night.

The set list was impossible to beat that night, from the first song, "Detroit Rock City," to the third encore, "Black Diamond." It was a candy store; it had everything I wanted, and it was there for the taking. The merchandise was amazing, too. In those days, you couldn't just click on a website and buy a shirt, you had to physically be at the show to get the special tour T-shirt. Believe me, I spent all my money.

I saw Kiss so many times as the years passed. I saw them two nights in a row at the Garden in '77. We were like the *Stranger Things* group of kids. Kiss was the thing that brought us together. On the Dynasty Tour in 1979, a bunch of us showed up in Kiss face paint and the full costumes. Charlie was Gene, I was Paul, my friend Frank was Peter, and my friend Peter was Ace. Charlie's a great artist and he did our makeup perfectly. We wore the wigs and everything as a tribute to these heroes of ours. Everybody was saying how good we looked. That was one of the moments that made me want to be a musician and get onstage. I loved the way that felt, and I carried that on into my own music.

Entertainers want acknowledgement; we want the spotlight; that's why I play the stage. I love the feeling that I get of being one with the crowd. There's no drug like it, which is why we in Anthrax stayed pretty much straight and narrow. There's no drug that can produce that feeling. To this day, when you take that first step onstage, and you know you have the songs, and if you feel confident and competent as a musician, there's no feeling like it.

When that happens, I say to myself, "Watch this!" because I have to impress myself. I have to improve on the last show I played, and I tell myself how lucky I am to be able to do this, so I gotta bring it to another level this time. It's a total addiction and I love every part of it. That's the Kiss influence, right there.

Now, let me tell you how I met them. You're probably going to think this story is bullshit, but I swear to you right now that every word of what follows is 100 percent true and accurate.

Somehow, my good friend Tom had great information about where Kiss were and what they were doing. I don't know who his inside sources were, but we would find out things that other fans would never know about, like exactly where they were going to be at a particular time. For example, Tom would somehow know when the band were meeting at Bill Aucoin's management office downtown in New York City. He called a lot of people because he had a lot of connections. Where from? To this day, I have no idea.

He'd pick up the phone.

"Wait, they're gonna be there today?"

He'd turn to me and say, "It's on!"

School would be cut out immediately. Once we knew there was a Kiss meeting going on downtown, we'd get the bus from the Bronx to Manhattan, which took twenty-five minutes. When we got there, we'd wait outside the management office at Fifty-Seventh Street and Madison for five or six hours in the freezing cold—which sucked, believe me...but that's how obsessed we were. What's crazy is that nobody really knew what Kiss looked like back then, because they hadn't taken the makeup off in public, so the only way we knew it was them was by looking for tall guys in suits with long black hair. Who else looked like that?

Finally, Kiss would come out, and we'd ask them for an autograph. After we'd done this twenty times in a row, Gene started to get suspicious. He would say, "What are you doing here? How did you know we were going to be here?" He was smart, and he would always want to know how we got our information, which was understandable.

He'd say, "I don't understand how you knew we were here."

"Oh! Uh, well, Gene, we took a guess and we got lucky!" we would reply, in our high-pitched, prepubescent voices.

After meeting our heroes so many times, it stopped being about just meeting them. It became about finding out what they were doing next.

"What's the plan for Kiss?" we'd ask.

"What's your set list?"

"When do you start touring?"

We must have been a huge pain in the ass for them. Paul was friendly, but he used to shake hands and leave, but Gene would stick around. He would always give us all the information we needed. He'd literally stand there and list off all the tour dates for us.

Now, feel free to disbelieve this, if you like—but after a while, Gene actually got to know our names. Think about that. This was a man with millions of fans, and he remembered the names of these two teenage kids.

"Frank Bello," he'd say in a resigned voice. "What are you doing here again?"

By meeting them in person, and getting to know them a little, I felt that we had a personal connection to Kiss. Us, the little club of kids—the *Stranger Things* group of kids. We had this special time in our lives where we could go downtown at any given moment and meet our heroes. There's nothing better than that. Nothing.

I thank those guys with all my heart for being there, and for everything they did back then. They don't even know what they did for us. It was guidance at a time when we needed it, in the best possible way. I have nothing but good things to say about these men. They were my comic book superheroes in more than one way. They gave me drive and purpose. They made me aspire to be something bigger. That's the honest truth.

Now, if you think that story was crazy, you'll love this one. Let me tell you a completely insane Kiss story—something you'll never believe. I barely believe it myself, but it happened, I promise you.

In 1982, not too long after Kiss released *Creatures of the Night*, we found out that they were recording their next album, which ended up being *Lick It Up*, at Right Track Studios on Forty-Eighth Street in Manhattan. Of course, Tom and I went downtown and waited outside, because somehow we thought we might get inside and see them one more time. You have to admit, we had some chutzpah.

When we walked up to the door, practically crapping in our underwear with nerves, there was a bell you could ring to get inside, but I was too afraid to push the button. I knew I wanted to go inside and see if Kiss were there, but I was genuinely scared.

Tom had balls of steel, though, and rang the bell.

There was a click as the mic opened. "Right Track Studios, who is this?"

Right away, Tom says, "Hi! We're here to see Gene."

I couldn't fucking believe he said that. Who has that kind of courage? I looked up and saw there was a security camera above the door pointing down at us, too. Shit! We were going to get busted, I thought. There was no way they were going to let us in.

Bzzzz! The door unlocked.

Holy shit.

Now I was genuinely shit-your-pants terrified. Was I going to witness the wrath of Gene Simmons? I didn't want to get on the bad side of Kiss, because they were my heroes.

But Tom said, "Come on, come on!" and walked right in.

I was so scared. As I walked in after him, I felt like I was walking in molasses, like I was in a haunted mansion or something. We got into the elevator and went upstairs, and I couldn't believe any of this was happening. I was fucking sweating.

We stepped out of the elevator and oh my God, now we were actually in the studio. I knew we were not supposed to be here. I thought we were going to get arrested for trespassing, or beat up by security, or all of the above.

I remember very vividly what happened next.

I look around and nobody's in the studio. The reception desk is right in front of us, but no one's there.

We look right, and then we look left where a wall is partly blocking our view. All we can see is two cowboy boots sticking out horizontally from the end of a sofa. They obviously belong to someone who is lying on the sofa, watching TV.

So we walk a little closer—and of course it's Gene Simmons.

Gene looks up and sees us...and I remember the expression on his face to this day. He sighed, and his head sank forward in disappointment. He totally recognized us as soon as we walked in.

He says, "What are you doing here?"

We stutter in our little pathetic voices, "We just wanted to come and say hello."

He hits us with a speech. "Do I come into your living room, when you're relaxing, when I'm not invited? I don't understand how you can just come into somebody's place of work and do that."

Of course, I'm feeling horrible about this. You might as well rip out my heart, I felt so guilty for being here. Innocently, Tom comes right back with a totally heartfelt line: "Sure! You can come over any time you like."

Gene just smiles and brings out a plate of cookies that he's been snacking on.

"Do you want one?"

I can't believe the God of Thunder is offering me a snack. I automatically say, "No, thank you, Gene," because I didn't want to impose, but Tom speaks right up and says, "Sure—thanks." The balls on this guy!

Now, this is where it gets truly crazy, because Tom then says, "We're here because we wanted to hear the new stuff."

Gene ponders this for a second before replying.

"Would you like to hear a new song?"

I literally couldn't believe that these words were coming out of his mouth. Would we like to hear a new song? Would *we* like to hear a new song? This is where dreams are made, right? So, Gene calls up the engineer on the studio phone and says, "I have some friends here. Can you pull up 'Young And Wasted'?" That song was brand new, and it was being mixed right there at the time.

Gene tells us, "Go inside and tell me what you think of the song," so in we go, and we sit down. I swear, I thought I was dreaming. The engineer plays "Young And Wasted," which was a great fucking song and blows us away because it's really heavy. The drummer Eric Carr, God rest his soul, absolutely killed it on that track.

We come out and Gene says, "Did you like it?" and of course we shout in our little high voices, "It's fucking great! It's fucking great!"

He nods and says, "So, I've given you what you want. Can I get back to work now?"

We walked to the elevator and I was floating on air, I swear. We had heard new Kiss music before anyone else in the world. We got in the same elevator that I had been so terrified in on the way up, and now we were on cloud nine on the way down. It was freezing cold on the way home, but I didn't even feel it.

Think about what Gene did for us, his fans, that day. He didn't have to do any of that. He knew how special it would be for us to have that experience, and so he gave it to us.

We couldn't wait to tell all our friends, and of course they didn't believe that any of that had happened, but we didn't give a fuck. It happened.

Later, when Anthrax got successful, I'd meet Gene from time to time and his opening line would always be, "Frank Bello, you're a powerful and attractive man," which was always hilarious. For that to happen to a guy who came from where I came from, that is huge.

Anthrax opened a lot of Kiss's *Crazy Nights* tour dates in 1988, and we'd walk into the stage area before sound check to see Gene, with one of our guitars, going through Kiss songs for a huddle of musicians. We'd call out songs and he'd say, "Well, this song comes from this, and this part comes from that." He'd play a Beatles song and say, "That inspired this Kiss song," and we'd all realize that it made sense, because Kiss were huge Beatles fans. We did that little group session quite a few times. After that I'd watch them sound check. Can you imagine anything cooler than watching Kiss jam on songs by Led Zeppelin or whatever?

Perhaps the craziest thing of all is that Gene still remembers our little *Stranger Things* gang, lining up for autographs back in the seventies. I asked him about it once, and he said, "I remember those days. You were there all the time. You were annoying sometimes, but it all worked out."

3
Into the Madhouse

S o HERE I AM, living it up in New York in the early eighties. Let's talk about what the city was like back then.

You've seen old New York in Martin Scorsese films, right? Well, I lived right there. I am that guy. I had the duck's-ass haircut like my friends the guidos, because that's what was popular back then. I probably sound like an old man, saying this stuff, but I am one, so that's okay.

Truth be told, I miss the seventies and the eighties. I know there was a lot of seediness and crime in New York back then, but man, you want to talk about the grit and character of the city? It was all there, back then. That was the real New York to me. I understand that the crime and the violence of that time was bad, I get that, and how sleazy and dirty and dangerous it could be—but at the same time, there's something to be said for all that.

Those were conservative times, and there was a lot of poverty, but there was something about the way that people respected each other. People had love for each other and wouldn't hammer you down the first thing you said. Nowadays people are ready to jump on you. I see it in New York every day.

Once in a while I'm confronted by a dickhead. I used to think, "I'm gonna kill this motherfucker," because that's my first instinct after the way I grew up, but nowadays I just defuse the situation. It's the only way that makes sense. I've seen a lot of stupidity in my life, as everybody has, and I've seen some stupid fighting as well, some of which I've been involved with. I'm no tough guy, I want to make that clear, but I've been involved in some fights that I've regretted later on. Usually it was because my friends got into a fight and I wanted to help them. I just don't want to see anybody hurt.

I really sound like an old geezer now, but there was a different flavor back then because there was more heart, and right now there's none of that in the city. It's really sad to see that all the stores I used to know are gone. There was history there among the seediness, and all that history got ripped out by young money. It really hurts when I see all this.

The big corporations came in with all this money and bought everything up. I saw it all happen in the eighties and into the nineties. I thought parts of it were great: the city is much cleaner, and it's a nicer place to visit from that point of view, but when they bought up all the theaters and Forty-Second Street changed completely, the city lost its character. All the mom-and-pop stores were moved out, which saddens me more than anything. It was the same with record stores and all the cool little places you could go to.

It's still happening now. Tech money bought Manhattan and cleaned it up, so everybody got moved out. They knocked down buildings and built huge new ones with no soul. When I go to Manhattan now, I don't recognize it. I rarely go there, in fact, unless it's for a business meeting or a night at the theater with my wife. I don't enjoy it there. Yes, nobody wants to get mugged, I understand that, but at the same time the character is no longer there. It got ripped out by people who just wanted to live there because they thought it was cool.

Fuck that. Give me my New York back!

Of course, that's never going to happen, so what do I do? I watch old movies with scenes of old New York. Martin Scorsese films have so much sweetness and passion for that era, and Robert De Niro has lived downtown forever. I've been in his neighborhood, and he tries to keep that going. I love that about him.

When he and Scorsese do films together, they get the little things right. I'll rewind those films just to see those details. Those things will stay with me forever. When I watched *The Irishman*, I had to watch it twice to appreciate it, because the first time was so emotional for me. It felt like I was saying goodbye to old friends, because I didn't know if I would ever see this group of great actors together again in a New York setting.

I realize that because I watch so many old films, I basically live in a fantasy land, but I do it because those films are a bubble of safety that I like. I always say that I was born in the wrong time because I appreciate the time when people cared about each other more.

I care a lot about people. Even if you're a dick to me, I'm still gonna talk to you and try to get around it. I'd rather people just gave each other a second, rather than being ready to pounce all the time. It drives me crazy.

Like I say, I know things were dangerous back then. I was on the bus almost every day when I was growing up in the Bronx. You had to keep your eyes open, because you never knew when a fight was going to blow up around you. You stepped on someone's shoe, you were in big trouble. I know all that. But once again, the city had heart. Believe me, I saw it. I lived it.

•••

MEANWHILE, BACK IN 1983 I'm having a ball, especially because I'm surrounded by so much cool music. You know I love Rush, and you know I love Kiss, but would you believe that I love Barbra Streisand, too? She's been one of my all-time favorite singers since I was a kid, and I still don't think she can be touched by anyone. I can listen to her in my headphones right now and she'll take me to a better place.

I know it sounds weird coming from a metal guy, but for sheer quality of tone, there is no voice like hers. Listen to "Somewhere" or "Evergreen," and you'll hear how she knows exactly how to hit those pressure points, where the melody peaks. When I have a shit day, I'll go back to those old Streisand songs because there's something in them that alleviates all of the stress. The music is absolutely glorious. It's almost orgasmic. I can say that, right?

For me, it's about more than just enjoying Barbra's music. Like I told you before, when I was a kid, my mom and dad would have some brutal fights. I love my mother with all my heart, but I don't think even she can understand what it's like to be a kid in the middle of an argument like that, with all the screaming. You don't realize the impact it has, and I take that very seriously around my son. My wife and I don't fight. I'm not doing that. Sure, we have disagreements, but we talk them out and then it's done.

Back then, Barbra was a buffer between me and the pain, an oasis of security. When there was an argument—and as I say, there were some ugly ones—I used to put a shield up by putting headphones on, and Barbra was my way out, my safe home. The voice that she had and the tones that she hit made everything all right, because I didn't have to hear the arguments.

Now you'll understand why I paid an unreasonable amount of money, like $700 or something, for my wife and I to see Barbra play at Madison Square Garden on her comeback tour in 2000. Crazy, right? It was incredible—the second-best gig of my life, after Kiss in 1977.

In the late seventies, all the great bands were right there for the taking. Cheap Trick were huge for me because they wrote great songs. We saw them just about everywhere. We got to know those guys, too, because we showed up so often.

We weren't as annoying with them as we were with Kiss, because Kiss were our hometown guys and we could easily go down and see them, but Cheap Trick were still really important to me because they really developed me as a musician. I still tell their singer Robin Zander to this day that he's one of the best rock-and-roll vocalists ever, hands down. I think he's underrated—he doesn't get the credit that he deserves, even though he can sing just about anything—and he's a great songwriter.

After Rush and Kiss, my tastes got heavier. I got into Motörhead through Charlie, and after that I got into Iron Maiden, who were huge for me. I have a great story about their bassist, Steve Harris. They were mixing their album *Piece of Mind* in early 1983 at Electric Lady Studios in Manhattan, and we heard that they were down there. Can you guess what happened next? Yep, we went down there to see what was happening, hoping that maybe they would invite us in. Again, looking back, I can't believe the balls we had to do that.

So, we walked right up to Electric Lady Studios and told them who we were and that we wanted to say hi to Steve, but they knew better than that, and said he was working. Of course, we decided to wait outside in case he came out. This was in Greenwich Village and there were loads of great little restaurants around, so we went around the corner to get a coffee and some food.

As we look through the window of this one restaurant, who do we see? It's Steve Harris, sitting by himself at a table in the restaurant, eating his dinner.

"Fuck! It's Steve! There he is!" we whisper to each other, standing there and staring at him. We didn't shout at him, or be a pain in the ass or anything, because we didn't want to bother him, but get this—he was facing the window, and he saw us standing outside. He could see that we were freezing, because our breath was making steam. It was bone-chilling cold outside, believe me.

Now, this is why Steve Harris is one of the best human beings on this Earth: he sees us, and he waves for us to come inside. He was still eating, but he says, "How are you, mate?" and we ask him about the album, which he says is coming along great. Then he says, "Have a seat!" and holy shit, now we're sitting down with Steve Harris.

Like Gene did, Steve took the time to be with his fans, and I will never forget that. It was moments like that which taught me how to treat people. There's no need to be a rock star in that situation: just be a human being to people. I learned right then that you have to take an extra second, no matter who the hell you think you are, to talk to people. I've carried that with me my whole life since then.

A funny detail is that, aside from being an influence on the bass, Steve has helped me out in another, unexpected way over the years. Every now and again I get digestion issues as a result of the shit food we get when we're on tour, and believe it or not, Steve helps me out with those whenever I see him. He's very educated on that subject, and he's given me tons of literature on what causes stomach ailments and advised me about the right nutrition and so on. You couldn't make this up, right?

So by 1983 I was quite the teenage headbanger. Saxon's *Denim and Leather* was another big album for me because it's fucking brilliant all the way through. I still listen to it today. All these great records are part of the scrapbook of our lives because they take you back to the first time you heard them. That whole wave of British metal was special because it was our thing. You didn't hear it anywhere else.

I love metal, of course, but more than that I love music, as you know because I just told you how much I love Barbra Streisand. In the very short lifetime that we have, why would anyone deny themselves the gift that is music? Whether you play it or you listen to it as a fan, why would you hold back from any part of it? Classical music, too: Tchaikovsky has so much beauty in it. We get to hear and enjoy that music and give our aural tastebuds that flavor.

In the meantime, between going to school and trying to hang out with the musicians that I admired, I was jamming a lot with Charlie. I played guitar first: I bought an old Telecaster copy and signed up for lessons at a local music store because I thought you needed to have lessons to learn, which of course is bullshit. I soon found out that lessons weren't for me.

Those lessons cost thirty-five dollars per hour, which was a lot of money for a kid who earned two bucks an hour at a deli, and I felt the teacher wasn't teaching me what I needed to learn. I showed him that I could already play chords, but for some reason he made me do lessons at a total beginner level, just so he could get more of my money. I hated that and quit after three or four lessons.

After that, I just taught myself by listening to the records that I liked. Charlie saw me playing one day and commented, "You're playing all the bass parts from the songs. Why don't you just switch to bass?" so we put together this beat-up, no-name Frankenstein bass and I started playing it. As soon as I played it, I knew it was for me.

Later I got a 1972 Fender Jazz, which I bought off a friend for $250, having saved all my deli earnings. That's when everything locked in for me because I could listen to a song and hear the bass part straight away. Like I told you, I'd buy records and learn the bass parts on the weekend instead of going out to the club with my guido buddies.

As music started to take over my life, I started to hang out with musicians at school. From ninth grade I went to Lehman High in the Bronx, where I was happy. All the bullies had gone away, so I was a good student at school and got good grades. I was a jokester, as I am now, but it was never malicious. School was a stressful fucking time, and I did enjoy the attention I got from being funny, but I also didn't want that to get in the way of my education. I knew I had to get my education done if I was ever going to get away from the poverty I'd experienced as a kid.

I was friends there with the Tempesta brothers Mike and John, who later became successful musicians. I remember me and Mikey cut school one day because the teacher was a sub and we thought, "Fuck this." He and I were just hanging out, outside the school, talking about Judas Priest, and this guy with a camera walks up to us out of nowhere and says, "Hey, do you mind if I take a picture of you guys behind the school? I like your leather jackets." We said yes, and I shit you not, the next day we were in *The New York Times*, as part of a story about students cutting out at New York schools. There was a whole piece on us.

Another time, I was supposed to go bowling with the school, but I didn't feel like it, so a few of us went to a diner nearby. Suddenly, a whole bunch of cops came in, took us out, and made us sign forms saying that we'd cut school. It wasn't an arrest, but it felt like it. That kind of thing happened quite a lot. They told my aunt about it, but I didn't really get into trouble because I worked hard and my grades were always great.

In May 1983, things took a step up when Charlie auditioned for a band named Anthrax. Their guitar player Scott Ian and their bassist Danny Lilker came over to our house to try him out. He set up his drum kit on a riser in this very small room at the top of the house. Believe it or not, Tina said "go for it" when Charlie asked her if it was okay to do that—even though the neighbors, who were nice people, would sometimes bang on the wall nonstop because the drums were so loud. All credit to my grandmother for that.

Now, I didn't know Scott and Danny at the time, so I stayed downstairs, out of the way. I could hear them and Charlie playing, though, and it was so fucking loud: there was a full-on metal production up there, even though it was the daytime. The house was rumbling from top to bottom. I was actually intimidated by how loud it was because all I'd done was play bass in my room with my little practice amp.

I really wanted Charlie to have his moment. I was pulling for him, and I was hoping that he'd get the Anthrax gig because I knew how important it was for him: he really wanted to join the band. I also knew how great he was as a drummer. He'd put in the time to get good, and he'd become a quintessential musician, a genuinely huge talent.

Of course, he got the gig, and I was so proud of him. I love the fact that it was in our home where Anthrax really began. For that magic to happen there, with Charlie getting in the band, I was so proud. That's how special this house was to me.

Once he was in Anthrax and rehearsing regularly with them, I used to hang around with them and help out. It's been said that I was a roadie, but it wasn't a paid job or anything: really, I just lugged gear because I didn't know shit. Charlie would ask me to fix a cymbal correctly, and I had no idea how to do it. I helped Danny with his bass gear, I guess, but I didn't know much about it; I could change strings, but not that well. Anyway, back then we didn't change strings unless they were broken because there was no money.

What we really did was just hang out and bust each other's balls; that was a great group of sarcastic motherfuckers, and I loved it.

We used to go to other bands' shows together, too: Scott and I used to go to Sunday matinees at CBGBs. I was a metal guy coming to the punk rock shows, but I loved the incredible energy, which was untouchable.

It was a great time for music because it was so raw. I just wanted to learn because I was so appreciative of the rawness of it all. I remember going in the pit, and not knowing what to do when I was in there. I guess I did whatever mosh I had learned how to do, but I was respectful because I didn't want to get in anybody's way. If I saw somebody fall, I'd help them up immediately. That's what you do. Metal and hardcore fans are smart and they're good people.

In July 1983, I turned eighteen and I started to take life more seriously. What was I going to do with my life? Whatever it was, I was going into it 100 percent, fully committed.

College was an option, although believe me, there was no money to go to college, and no scholarship or anything like that, so my plan was to go to community college if I had to and see what I could make of it. There was also baseball, which I loved, but I didn't know if I was good enough to get a scholarship.

What I really wanted to do with my life, of course, was to play music. That's what I yearned to do, if I could just find the right opportunity. I knew Anthrax was recording a debut album, *Fistful of Metal*, and that they were going to play live dates in 1984. I thought that going on tour with them as a roadie would be a great way to get into the industry, so I said to myself, "If I crap out of the music thing, I can always go back to college later on."

That was my plan. No matter what happened, I was going to work my hardest. I was going to put everything into whatever I did. Music was the first thing that I tried, so I gave it everything, but I would have given it all, whatever I did.

You could call this confidence, but the reality is that it was a necessity for me. I refused to live in poverty anymore. My aunt and my grandmother gave me everything I could ask for, but I never had any money that was mine. I always remembered when my mother and I were on welfare, and the feeling in the pit of my stomach that I felt back then, and I swore I was never going to feel that again. I feel for anybody who has been in that situation, and I'll help anybody who needs advice about how to get out of it. The answer is that you have to go all in. There's no other way to do it.

The only problem in the way of me going on tour with Anthrax in '84 was that I still had a semester of school to finish. Fortunately, I saw that some kids at my school were graduating early thanks to a special program where you could double up your credits and finish six months before everybody else. By doubling up all the credits I would have needed in that second half of the year, if I really buckled down, I could do it.

It was all making sense to me now that I knew what I wanted to do, so I worked my ass off through 1983 so I could finish in the following January. All credit to my high school for instilling the idea in me that I was responsible for my own work. If you wanted to get things done, you worked hard, which I did—and it made all the difference to my career.

Everything changed for me one day in early 1984, right before I graduated high school. My friend Tom called me up and said, "Hey, Frank, you might want to learn some Anthrax songs."

"Why?" I asked.

"Because you might be jamming to them."

A couple of days later, Charlie asked me to come in and audition for Anthrax at their rehearsal place.

Now, I had heard rumors that Danny Lilker might be leaving the band, but I stayed out of all that. I didn't want to know the details of what was happening, because I love Danny—he's a great bass player and songwriter. It was very hard to consider taking his place because he was a friend of mine and I really liked him. At the same time, I thought that if there was an opening for a bass player in Anthrax, I'd rather it be me than someone else because I knew I could do it. Why have a stranger come in?

So here I was, auditioning for Anthrax, right there in front of the four other guys, who were the singer Neil Turbin, the guitar players Scott Ian and Danny Spitz, and Charlie on drums. It didn't feel like a formal audition, more like a jam session, but I was still very intimidated.

I didn't have a big bass cabinet or anything; before that, I was just playing in my room. I'd never been in a band. All I'd done was jam with Charlie at home on Rush, Maiden, and Kiss songs. My friend Mike came over and jammed on guitar, too, which was cool, but it was hardly solid band experience.

Shit, I can't even explain how scared I was.

I want you, reader, to understand what it was like. Imagine being eighteen like I was, not knowing much, coming from your bedroom—literally, your bedroom—to jam in a live situation. You've been around live music for a while, but you've never actually taken the step onto the stage. This was a professional band, too, made up of older guys who were all incredible musicians, and let's not forget, Anthrax had a record deal already. In 1984, a record deal was almost unthinkable for a kid like me.

Of course, I was close to Charlie, which took some of the nervousness away because I felt comfortable around him and I knew he was pulling for me—but I still had to play the fucking songs. I knew them like the back of my hand, but the question was whether I could step into that circle and be as intense as they were. Could I keep up? Could I thrive?

To get through it, I just put my head down, played the songs, and headbanged. I knew it went well because the vibe was good afterward. Neil told me, "You did fucking great!" after the audition, which gave me a boost of confidence—and then they told me I was in, and I couldn't believe what I was hearing. I had never felt so excited in all my life.

The day that *Fistful of Metal* was released was my first official day as a member of Anthrax. Holy shit. It was time to step up.

4
Armed and Diseased

M Y FIRST SHOW AS a member of Anthrax was on February 25, 1984, at L'Amour's in New York. Here's what I remember.

All my family and all my friends were there. You can imagine the big hoopla. I was so nervous, because L'Amour's was the rock capital of New York. I thought to myself right before we went on, "I think I remember the songs, so I'm just gonna go for it. If I fuck up, I fuck up: I'll cover it," because I had to calm myself down. Look it up on YouTube and you'll see footage of this gig. I had short hair at the time, and I couldn't wait to grow it long so I would fit in.

Being onstage for the first time is a bit like fucking for the first time. You don't really know what you're doing, so you just go for it. You've read the books and studied the videos, so you just jump in and try to do what others have done before you. It really is like the first time you have sex: you're like, "Okay, I'm going in and I'm gonna try my best!" At the same time, you don't want to blow your entire load in the first five minutes. Nice metaphor, right?

So, you can imagine the intensity of that first show for me, and having that crowd there, and not really knowing what to do, although I knew how to play the songs. Once again, like I did in the audition, I just headbanged as well as I could.

In the first song, "Deathrider," I headbanged particularly hard. *Crack...*

I literally heard something snap and felt a sudden burning in the back of my neck.

"What the hell is that?" I thought in a panic. "You can't stop now!"

I just kept going, repeating to myself, "I'll go to the hospital later...I'll go to the hospital later." That's how bad the burning was. Thank God it went away a few songs later, or I don't know what would have happened to my brand-new career as a musician.

I recently watched that show on YouTube, and you want to know what my favorite part of it was? Not the actual show, but the backstage footage of us before the show, with all the banter and ballbusting between us. We were on a mission to see what this band could do. We didn't know what our goal was, we just wanted to push forward as far as we could.

That video reminded me of how the ballbusting—which was basically attacking each other's weak points with sarcasm, in a friendly, harmless way—got us through the bad days and the dead space. We'd find ways to fuck with each other, and we really got to know each other that way. That made us tight, as friends, before we even got onstage.

We weren't just passing the time with all this mutual sarcasm—we men actually bond that way. That's because ballbusting is a test of how much you can handle. It really is all about being the dominant male, and all that stupid stuff. You find yourself thinking, "How much can this guy take?" because it reveals a lot about his personality. You find out a lot about each other, and where each other's head is at—whether you can't fuck with one guy too much, or whether he's good with it and comes right back at you. If he does that, it raises my game, and then all bets are off.

If you think about it, that was our only entertainment on the long van journeys between gigs in 1984 and '85, because there was nothing else to do. We all knew each other so well that we always looked for any kind of weakness, and then we blew it up. I don't think anybody in Anthrax escaped it, because everybody had their thing. Mine was that I looked like a guido from the Bronx, because I didn't have long hair yet, even though I was playing in a metal band.

This is where the trust between us began, because we knew each other's personalities so well, and that trust went with us onto the stage. Also, in those days our crew was made up of our friends, and they were chiming in, too. All of us were part of the same bunch of idiots, having a really good time.

The early Anthrax shows taught me how to be a performer onstage and how to react to the energy coming from the crowd. To handle that energy, I went back to my heroes. I thought, *This is what Steve Harris would do; This is what Geezer Butler would do; This is what Geddy Lee would do.*

Steve Harris would put his foot onto the monitor and play to the crowd; Geezer would jam over at the side; Geddy would concentrate on the music. I was going through the files in my memory, right there onstage. All of my heroes, and all of my growing up with them, was right there on the stage at my first show. I relied on them to pull me through, and they didn't let me down.

We did a lot of touring in 1984, playing our own dates and also with the British band Raven. It was pretty insane. We got to know Raven pretty well; the singer and bassist John Gallagher is one of the sweetest people I've ever met.

I didn't really know what being in a band meant, at first. I knew we'd go on tour, but I assumed that we'd be traveling on a tour bus and all that stuff. Of course, we traveled in a van, right across the country, which was exhausting, but I didn't care because I was so young and so excited. We'd stop to eat, and then the road trip would continue. I didn't even have my driver's license yet, only my temporary one, so everyone was afraid to let me drive, understandably.

Of course, there was no money. My mom helped me to get my first Jackson bass. She gave me half the money for it because I didn't have enough for it from the money I made in the deli. We weren't making a lot of money in Anthrax, of course. I remember how excited we were when we got our very first hotel room—a single room, for all the guys in the van. It was pandemonium. Constant farting, and all that stupid guy stuff.

Still, we took care of business in the right way. I signed up as a full member, with a one-fifth share of everything, no matter who wrote the songs. One thing I've always loved about this band is that we're all smart enough to know that everybody's split has to be equal. That way, if I'm busting my ass as hard as one of the other guys, I'm not going to feel weird that he's getting paid more than me. Whatever money came in, we split it equally, and that kept the band together. It was a very smart move, right at the beginning of the band.

Jon Zazula was Anthrax's manager from the beginning. I've always been close with him and to his late wife Marsha, who passed away when I was writing this book. They were very nurturing and helpful, especially in those early days. They always looked after me and gave me confidence, and I love them for that. They thought I was good for Anthrax, and I thank them for it.

My family was pleased that I joined Anthrax because I was with Charlie, and they wanted us to stay together. My mom never stopped worrying about me, though. I'll never forget a show in Pittsburgh, Pennsylvania. Life had taken over, so I hadn't called her in a few days, and—because I'm from such a tight-knit family—what did she do? She got on a plane and flew out to Pittsburgh because she hadn't heard from me. God bless her, I love her to death for it, of course, but you can imagine how embarrassed I was when she walked in, right in front of the other guys. They were like, "Dude, why's your mom here?" and I said, "Because I forgot to call her."

I asked, "Mom, what are you doing here?"

She said, "I wanted to make sure you were okay."

"Mom, you can't do this. These are my friends!"

"But I didn't hear from you! You didn't call!"

I sighed and said, "All right, Mom," and let it slide. You have to cut your losses in that situation and accept it. She stayed for the whole show and at the end I said, "Thanks for coming, Mom, I love you. Please never do this again!" like the ungrateful idiot I was. It was all good, but it taught me a lesson: stay in touch with the people who love you. She got her point across.

I'll always remember opening for Metallica and Raven at the Roseland Ballroom in New York on August 3, 1984. It was a great, big, famous place to play, and it was old-school New York with that special vibe. A lot of people were there, and it felt like a pivotal show for Anthrax. It was doubly intense because it was our hometown.

I'd known Metallica for a year or so at this point. They worked fucking hard, as we all do. They went through the trenches, wearing the same clothes every day, like we did. The first time I met Cliff Burton was when Scott introduced me to him, and I quickly became a fan of Cliff's bass playing: he was doing unheard-of things with the bass that I loved. It was so left field of everything that I'd grown up on, and I was fascinated by the sounds he made, because you didn't think a bass could make those sounds. He was a great physical player: he had the full package of techniques, but he had that crucial extra element—a voice on the bass.

When Cliff played, you knew it was him, because there was character in his playing. He could make sounds that no other bass player could make. He was an artist on bass, for me, and he really painted a picture with his instrument. Sometimes I'll play part of his solo, "(Anesthesia) Pulling Teeth," and think, "What was Cliff thinking when he wrote this part?" and break it down note by note and think, "Look what he did there!"

I fucking love that, because it's a way to be with Cliff, which is the only way to do it in his absence. As he played the bass, his beautiful character came through to you, and that's what made him unique. There was so much stuff he played live that you didn't hear on the records, because Metallica's sound was all about drums and guitars.

The Roseland show in August '84 was where Metallica got signed to Elektra. We knew that the record company people were coming down, and every band on that bill was on fire for that reason, but Metallica in particular kicked ass—and it was great to watch. It was everything that those early days of thrash metal were about. You wanted to be a part of it because you knew that it was an opportunity for these three bands to make a mark together.

When all the businesspeople come to hear the music you're making, you know that things are about to elevate. This music was going to catapult into the mainstream, with money behind it to make more people hear it. You could feel that this was going to happen. We all felt that the music was different, and that it was enough to be a movement. The energy was unlike anything else: it was the next step for metal.

We really felt like we were on some kind of ride. That one show really demonstrated that the music was now coming of age. It felt to me like the beginning of a new era, and I was proven right about that, because after that it just kept right on going, and getting bigger and bigger.

These early times in Anthrax came with their fair share of ups and downs. There was a lot of comedy, some incidents more palatable than others. I remember I got some very expensive leather pants, and they were very uncomfortable and stank like a motherfucker. After a week wearing those things, they smelled like a mixture of shit, piss, and mildew. It didn't matter what I did. I could hang them up in the van to dry out, and they still fucking reeked. It was the worst smell in the world, and I had to put them on, night after night.

There was drama, too, and sometimes it could be stressful. Everybody had personality conflicts at one time or other, but most of the time we got through it as a band. Those van journeys were all about ballbusting, as you can imagine. We all did it to each other. All this New Yorker stuff must have been annoying, but my God, it was the funniest time ever.

Neil asked me to wear chain mail onstage, but I didn't like it because it was so heavy. I was new in the band, and I didn't want to cause any waves and be a pain in the ass. I decided to be a team player and wear the chain mail, but man, it was rubbing against my skin and giving me cuts and a rash.

A couple of weeks after the Roseland show, Neil was no longer our singer. It was hard, because he helped me when I joined, but at the same time I knew it needed to happen for the future of the band. It was nothing against Neil at all; it was one of those business decisions that you sometimes have to make.

Unfortunately, I fought a lot with Charlie over the years. Of course, I love him, but he and I have been through the mill together, fighting as brothers do. There's been some crazy times, but they've all been for the good of Anthrax. I believe the tension between us when we're writing together helps the intensity of our music. I don't know why. Maybe it's because us being on edge gets put into the music, somehow. It works.

Sometimes it got physical. Nobody was pulling out knives and guns, but we would get into it with fists. I remember throwing a skateboard at Charlie, and he threw a chair back. It was one of those classic Frank and Charlie fights. One time we had a talcum powder fight in the kitchen at my grandmother's house. He and I had got into it over something really stupid that I've forgotten. There was a big container of talcum powder, and somebody threw it onto somebody. Then another one showed up, and we started throwing powder everywhere.

We ran outside and there was powder out there, too. We were completely covered because we were going at it pretty fucking good, wrestling in this talcum powder. Somebody broke us up. I remember it as a lot of fun—a fun, stupid fight. After these things, one of us would apologize and say "I'm sorry, that shit shouldn't have happened," and it was always cool after that, until the next time.

So there were issues here and there in 1984, but come on, it was a great year for me. Anthrax was my next move in life—my going to college, if you like—and I felt very fortunate. I knew that education wasn't in my future when I made that choice, which was scary because I knew I would need a job a few years ahead if the band didn't work, and a decent job would need me to have been to college.

In other words, Anthrax had to work out for me. I had to make it work. I'd had a taste of the good stuff and, like an addict, I wanted more. I needed to be in this band nonstop, 24/7, and I wanted to push it forward, as did all the other guys. Our drive was huge. We didn't know what the next step was. In fact, it's good not to know what the next step is. Whatever it was, we were determined to take it.

···

AT THE BEGINNING OF 1985, my life basically consisted of rehearsing, playing shows, and working at Joe's Deli when I was home. I look back at that now, and I laugh at how simple a life that was. I had no money because Anthrax didn't really make any at this point, so I just earned a few bucks at the deli, played bass, and was happy. There's a lot to be said for that kind of easy, focused existence.

Without a singer, we considered continuing as a four-piece, with Scott doing harsh vocals and me doing a clean style. It would have been like the Paul Stanley and Gene Simmons thing, although I think neither Scott nor I really wanted to do it. I was still young, and I didn't feel I could handle vocals as well as play bass. In fact, I felt lucky to be playing bass in Anthrax at all. I was still finding my feet as a man and as a musician.

Still, I sometimes wonder what we would have sounded like with that lineup—no disrespect to our later singers Joey Belladonna and John Bush, both of whom I love dearly and who have some of the greatest voices I've ever heard. It would have been an interesting dynamic. We wouldn't have done it half-assed, that's for sure. With the way we care about everything, we would have really taken our time over it, taken it apart and made sure it was done right. But the better thing to do was find someone who was the right fit as a front man, like my favorite groups all did. It was a fun little thought.

After that discussion, we knew we wanted to find a great singer. That was the plan. A guy named Matt Fallon was our singer for a short time. He didn't stay long, because he wasn't what we needed for the vocals. It had to be right, because we're die-hard fans of this music ourselves, and unless it's right we would never put it out. That stands to this day.

By now we were putting together an EP, *Armed and Dangerous*, and our producer Carl Canedy recommended Joey Belladonna to us. I remember when Joey came to the audition, he was wearing red leopard-print jeans with boots of some kind. We were T-shirt and jeans guys, and he clearly came from a different school, but look, it all contributed to the magic of Anthrax. His singing was great and he knew a wide range of songs, which really helped us. He has what I think of as a classic rock voice, which was the cherry on top of the metal songs that we recorded, and that's what separated us from the other bands.

We still sound different to this day, and I'm proud of that, not just as the bass player in Anthrax, but as an Anthrax fan. Joey comes off as a soft-spoken introvert when you speak to him, but he's also one of the nicest people on the planet, with a big heart.

It was scary recording the *Armed and Dangerous* EP. Hell, that whole time was very scary. I was nineteen, and I'd come from playing bass in my bedroom along with vinyl records to a professional situation. Think about that. I was thinking, "Oh, my God, this is a recording studio. There's a producer." All these thoughts were in my head. "I'm actually going into a studio to record!"

I'm proud of myself, though, because I loved pressure. I've always been a high-wire act, metaphorically speaking; I love standing on the high-wire and seeing what happens. I say, "Fuck yeah! Let's see what happens." Also, I couldn't contemplate failure. Remember, failure didn't exist for me. I was going to improvise anything I could do that I learned, and if you listen to those early songs, you'll hear all the influences that I have on bass. They were all I had to rely on—Geezer, Steve, and Geddy—but they never let me down.

If that EP was a scary experience, recording my first full-length album, *Spreading the Disease*, was ten times worse. I was fucking terrified. I was really under the microscope now, with our producer Carl—whose band The Rods I loved, like everyone did—looking at me. All I could think was, "I only know how to record bass in my room." Even then, I only recorded to cassette tape, I didn't know what the fuck I was doing. I didn't know the studio procedure at all.

In the studio, some of the other guys were in there watching me, which made me even more nervous, because they'd recorded a full album before and I hadn't. I'm thinking, "What if I forget the songs? What if they don't like my bass parts and I have to do them again?" All these scary thoughts were flooding into my head, like they do when you're inexperienced at anything.

I look down at my right hand and I see that it's started to shake. Out of nowhere, it started to do that. Why? It never did that before. Carl sees this and goes, "You okay, Frank?" which makes me feel even worse, because now I know he's onto me and he knows that I'm shitting my pants.

But this is where Carl reveals what a genius he is, because he takes me into the kitchen and gives me a shot of whiskey. That was clever, because not only did the whiskey made me feel warm and relaxed, but it also let me know that he was on my side. It was a great head game that he played there, and a great producer trick that really worked, because now I felt that everything was going to be okay—and when that's your attitude, then everything probably *is* going to be okay.

It flowed from there. I thought to myself, "Just go for it. Play what you want to play, and if Carl doesn't like it, let him edit it later, or I'll do it again." The first song I recorded was "Lone Justice," and there's a lot of bass in that song, so I mostly relied on Steve Harris for that song, with Geddy Lee second. They were all in there, because once again, that was all I knew.

Fortunately, Carl loved 90 percent of everything I played. I have to credit him, because he kept building me up. He was the first guy who made me feel, "Wow, I can actually do this at a professional level." Once the first song was done, then I had the confidence to keep going. I trusted him enough to bounce bass lines off of him. I'd say, "Is this too much?" because I never wanted to overplay for the song or be the annoying solo bass guy—I wanted to help the song to be better.

For a young bass player, I think I did fine. If you know the song "Gung-Ho," you'll know how fast it is. It would be a challenge for any bass player who plays fingerstyle, like I do, so I used a pick on that song. When I used my fingers, it didn't sound quite on the riff, because it was so intricate. It also sounded mushy, no matter how hard I tried, so I did what was good for the song. That bass part was done in a first take, which I'm proud of because first takes have that live feel that always sounds so great.

I was starting to develop a style of my own on bass, I guess, now that we were getting to know each other as recording musicians. When you play live, nobody really hears what you do on bass, so it was only on *Armed* and *Spreading* that the other guys really listened to my playing.

I was a bit possessive about my bass parts, now that I look back. If I thought the part was right, and it helped the vocal and it helped the song build in intensity, I would fight for it, even if the other members of Anthrax didn't agree. I think everybody in a band should do that, unless your part stands in the way of the song.

A band is a committee and everything has to work for everybody, so the arguments raged. Charlie or Scott often said, "That bass part is really fucking cool, Frank," but sometimes they would say, "No, it's too much." Because I was still young, I felt like they were trying to take something away from me, so I'd be like, "Fuck you! That's fucking staying in there. I didn't say anything about that fucking drum roll you did that lasted a half an hour."

Of course, I can express this in a more mature way these days, but at the time, it got personal, unfortunately.

Carl knew better than to get in the middle of this. He used to brush his teeth all day for some reason, so he'd be standing there with his toothbrush, brushing his teeth right in the middle of the session, and let us go at it. After a while, though, he'd have to put the referee shirt on and be objective about what was good for the song. That's when I learned when to fight the battle and when to pull back. This was how I understood what to do and what not to do in a band. I learned to compromise, but also to stand my ground, within reason.

Looking back, I see that being in Anthrax was great for my self-esteem. Growing up in the Bronx fatherless made me rely on myself, and it helped me find out who I was. My calling was music, and it still is. I'm not the most religious person, but I give thanks to God every day for music. I'm very fortunate to have it, because it took the place of all the pain I went through. It was my outlet, and still is. Any time I need solace, I'll listen to one of the artists who inspired me, or I'll pick up a guitar and play. It's how I get the bad feelings out of me.

For me, that works, and I believe anybody can use that outlet, especially kids who are going through a hard time. Music has been so good to me—why wouldn't I want to help somebody get to the place that they need to be? Whatever helped get me there, I want to pass it on to help you. You can have it, too, and I hope you'll create beautiful music.

5
Island Life

IN 1985, ANTHRAX DIDN'T feel like a business yet, but that changed soon afterward. I guess it started to feel like a real ongoing entity to me when Jonny Z signed us to Island Records as a joint venture with Megaforce, and we started getting paychecks. Jonny was our manager right up until 1995, which is a long relationship in this crazy business.

Talking of relationships, I had one long-term girlfriend, from around 1985 or so, that lasted for quite a few years. Out of respect, I won't mention her name, but it was rough on her because I was away a lot. Let me be very clear about this, though—I was never unfaithful to my girlfriend. I would never do that to someone I'm with, and this is God's honest truth, I never did it. I made a promise to myself that I wouldn't hurt anyone that way.

It was important to me because my parents split when I was young. I believe in commitment, and I believe in keeping my word. Life is so fucking short that it's important to keep your word. There is a bigger picture, and there is a mission to achieve. I don't want anything to be a bump in the road on the ride I'm on.

Anthrax had a vision—almost a tunnel vision—to get the main goal done. Our drive is a heart, a pulse, which beats to this day. Our goal is to make the band work. This goal has never been seriously threatened from my point of view, not even by S.O.D., the band that Scott and Charlie started right after we finished recording *Spreading the Disease.*

What happened was that those guys wanted to do a hardcore project on the side, with our buddy Billy Milano on vocals. Danny Lilker played bass on their album, *Speak English or Die.* I was glad that Danny got back together with Scott and Charlie—that alone was a very cool thing—but also, he was the better choice for that band than me. It didn't upset or offend me at all, as some people have assumed over the years, although I admit that I was nervous that Anthrax would be fractured by the new project.

We were on a great path, and now this other thing was competing with our band. Believe me, I'm a big fan of S.O.D., and I'm a big fan of Billy Milano, but I thought, "Why wouldn't we use these songs for our next album?" and, "Why would we distract our fans when we're on such a roll?" That's as honest as I can be about it.

Anyway, no harm was done because Anthrax was getting bigger and bigger as we rolled into 1986. When we signed to Island, we used to go down to the Island office on Fourth and Broadway in Manhattan, to this building where Cher and Keith Richards both lived at the time. We'd see them there—Keith would be walking his dog, and Cher would be getting into a limo.

We'd go up to the Island office, take meetings with them, and walk out with boxes of U2 and Bob Marley CDs from these huge cabinets that they had in there. Our main girl at Island was Janet Kleinbaum, and I love her like a sister. She truly cared about the success of Anthrax, and became like another family member because she always went to bat for us against the higher-ups at the record company. We were popular there because we were on our way up, and they saw dollar signs when they thought about Anthrax, of course, but it didn't feel as cynical as it sounds. It genuinely felt like a family at Island.

Fans were now starting to recognize us in the street and ask for autographs. When it was my turn, I just tried to be one of the guys, exactly as I'd learned from Steve Harris four years before. I didn't feel the need for fame or celebrity, I just wanted to talk to people. I had been the kid waiting to see his idol in the freezing cold, so I knew what it was like for those kids, and I made sure that they felt welcome.

In all the years since then, I've never said no to giving someone a signature or taking a picture with them. Why wouldn't you do that? It's part of the gig, but more than that, it's part of being a decent human. If you're lucky enough to be in this position, never forget where you came from.

This was such a great time for us. *Spreading the Disease* had turned out great, and now I wanted to see what came next, because there was a momentum building. I could feel it. A fire was burning under us, and when we started to play out live and gel as a band with our new singer, Joey, that was another important step forward.

We were now starting to understand what we were capable of, and each one of our personalities was starting to develop. It was a huge step in our evolution, as was the video we did for "Madhouse" around this time. The video isn't amazing or anything, but that's not the point. The simple fact of Anthrax doing a video, with where we came from and the kind of music we played, was practically unbelievable.

I was really happy, because I was doing what I wanted to do. There still wasn't much money, but it was coming soon, and anyway, it wasn't my goal to have money. It's still not my goal. All I want to do in this life is support my family, be healthy and happy, and have a decent life; I don't want or expect to be a billionaire. All I ever wanted was to go to the edge and see what was on the other side.

Believe it or not, we were signed to a major label and we were selling serious numbers of albums, but Uncle Joe's deli was what was keeping me alive. Joe let me have time off whenever I needed it because he knew this was what I wanted to do. It would have been impossible for me to make it work if he hadn't understood that and been so generous with me. From him to my mom to my grandmother, we were blessed: all of us in the band. If you're reading this as a parent, always be supportive of your children. Let them follow their dream. Never let them say, "I should have…"

Whether it paid well or not, I enjoyed working at the deli. All my friends hung out there, and my Uncle Joe was great. I guess I learned how to be a man from him because he was a father figure to me. He taught me a lot of lessons in life, so thank God for him. I could write a book about that deli, or even better, a TV sitcom, because it was full of characters who would come in and teach me about life from a very young age.

I even used to date girls who came in, some of whom were quite a bit older than me and taught me how to behave as a boyfriend. They'd come in after work at five o'clock in the afternoon, and I would always look forward to that. I learned my banter that way, and that would turn into a date.

These are all very New York stories. Imagine the accents, and the clothes, and the whole attitude. The guys would come in, and we'd drink coffee and talk bullshit about girls and life, and maybe about music, too. It was a great time, and I loved working there.

Well, most of the time. There was this one old lady who would come in, right before I closed up the deli so I could clean up the meat-slicing machine, and demand that I cut her a quarter pound of liverwurst. Now, for one, I didn't like to sell anything less than half a pound, because it was too small to bother with and it's a waste of time. Two, if you know what liverwurst is, you know it smells disgusting, like fungus. Three, this old lady would insist that I cut the liverwurst so thin that she could see through it, which is impossible because it breaks apart if you cut it that thin.

"I wanna see right through it!" she'd say, every fucking night when she came in. I'd be thinking, "You can't see through liverwurst. Why are you wasting my time? I want to go home!" but I still had to do it, and then clean the machine up right afterward. That kind of thing happened a lot.

One night, I was working at the deli and I needed a break, just to get out from behind the register and get a breath of fresh air, so I went out front for a minute. There were always guys hanging out there, like an old Scorsese movie. As I was standing there, this guy came flying down the street on a motorcycle and smacked into a van, right in front of me.

This poor guy didn't have a helmet, and his head was crushed. He died right on the spot. There was blood everywhere. I was only fourteen at the time, and it shocked me deeply. Since then, I've never ridden a motorcycle, because I've seen what can happen.

Death is always nearby. Ricky Gervais, who has a sharp edge to his comedy that I've always loved, says it best: he warns us that the time to get things done is now. He's unapologetic when he does an awards show, and he reminds the celebrities in the audience that they're all very rich and famous, but that they don't do anything that really benefits society. It's very real and honest, and he says it in a sarcastic way that appeals to my personality. I've been to the Grammy awards myself and I know that none of us there cured cancer or did anything really significant to help people.

And then some of these people have attitudes, which fucking kills me. Like, seriously? You're lucky enough to walk on a set and be pampered, when a lot of people can't even get a job, and you still have an attitude? I see all that stuff in a different light now. If people

FRANK BELLO

want an autograph or a picture, find the time to spend with them. If you can't do that, then fuck you.

My experiences with Gene Simmons and Steve Harris are my go-to memories when it comes to how to treat people; they're always on my mind. If I'm on a nice, warm tour bus in the middle of nowhere, and I see some kid waiting for an autograph and freezing his ass off, I realize that I was that kid, and I want to alleviate his pain. It makes no sense not to do that, just as a human being.

To continue this idea, I basically feel that I'm in debt to the people who made our band a success. I always feel that I have to make somebody feel the way that I do, because it pulled me out of the darkness that I was in. I don't want anybody to feel like that. I feel so lucky that I found this music, because it was my calling.

I say this at my clinics: if I can make one person feel like I do about music, which is an outlet for beauty and hope, my job is done. Music is the key to the door of a world of beauty—a gorgeous, deep world that I am forever grateful for. I want people to be open to all kinds of music because it will make you you. Music gives the world flavor.

While I'm delivering all this life advice, I think it's important to try to be a good human being. I think most people want to be good, deep down, but for some reason some people can't do it. But like I said, life is fucking short. I see this every day. You have to make the most of your time. Take advantage of every opportunity while you can.

All right, that's enough homespun Bello wisdom for now. Back to Anthrax.

After the Island deal, we started getting a salary. It wasn't a lot, but it helped. As for the wider thrash metal scene that we were part of, well, this music was coming up fast, and you had to jump on the high wire, walk out on it, and see what happened. Nobody knew what the fuck was going to happen tomorrow, but we believed that we had something special.

That became clear when we were asked to open for Black Sabbath in early '86. Shit, that was a huge compliment. We were pretty excited when we first heard about it, although that didn't last long because when we got on the tour, we were told right off the bat that ticket sales weren't good.

I should say that this wasn't the Black Sabbath that we knew from the old days, with Ozzy Osbourne as the singer. It wasn't even the Ronnie James Dio band. It was Tony Iommi, who has always been awesome to Anthrax, and is a big influence on all of us; plus Danny Spitz's brother, Dave, on bass; Eric Singer on drums; and Glenn Hughes on vocals.

I love Glenn; he's an incredible singer and bassist, the full package. Everybody treated us great, but the ticket sales weren't there, so we left the tour after we did four dates. The main thing I remember about that tour is that nobody was sure about anything. Nothing was concrete. They told us, "This might happen, and that might happen," but nothing did actually happen, and we weren't surprised when it ended.

We weren't too disappointed, actually. It was cool playing arenas because we were still a club band, but they weren't full by any means, and this wasn't the Black Sabbath I had grown up with. What's more, we had our first European tour coming up— and talking of that tour, I know the Cold War was in full flow in 1986, but I gotta say, I didn't expect my first trip to Europe to be accompanied by warnings about nuclear fallout.

Before the aptly titled US Speed Metal Tour in Europe, which ran from May 7 to May 29, I'd never been outside of America. In fact, I'd never been outside New York, unless you include New Jersey. Europe was totally unknown to me, and I was still only twenty years old when we flew over.

I was totally bright-eyed and bushy-tailed and had no clue. You think, "We're going on tour in Europe!" but you don't realize what you're actually going to do, or what it's actually going to be like when you get there. Thank God we were young and resilient.

I know we'd played a bunch of dates in America, but Europe just seemed like a whole other world to us. For me, it felt like I was coming out of the deli and jumping right into the great unknown. We felt like explorers. Now that I'm an old guy, I appreciate how fortunate I was to be doing it. Who does anything like that, especially with my background? This music had got me out of what I was doing into a whole new world that was opening up. I had the opportunity to fly over to Europe on someone else's dime and play shows to different people from different places. How fucking cool was that?

Not that I had this adult perspective at the time, of course. Back then I was just excited for the band, because we were moving on and up. Going on tour is still a big deal, even today. It's so fucking expensive to do, which was even more of a huge deal back then because we had no money and hardly anybody knew who we were. We didn't know if there would even be any crowds at the shows.

I will say this: we knew we were functioning well as a band, because we were friends before we were bandmates. That nucleus was there, so we were prepared to take on anything and anyone. You had to work hard to get exposure for your band back then, because there wasn't much music TV and radio for our kind of music. The only way your band was going to get bigger was to make people come and see you, and when they came, you had to be special.

My whole thinking was, "What do people love? People love energy, so give it to them." Fortunately, our music was all about energy, so we'd give it to them and that would get us through to the next day, and the next stage in our career.

Let me take you along with us. We and the opening bands Overkill and Agent Steel get on a plane, and we land, and right away I'm in the history books that I'd read at school. We play quite a few dates in Germany, which is great because I love that country, and immediately I'm forced to grow up, because I'm obsessed with food—and over there, the food is very, very different to what I'm used to. Compared with the food that my grandmother cooked at home, as the best cook in the world, the backstage food that we ate was terrible. We had no money, though, so that was all we ate.

They gave us these meat dishes that were covered in some kind of weird, neon-colored sauce. I swear, it was practically glowing bright red or pink. I don't know what the fuck it was, but it was never going down my throat. No way. It was also really burned a lot of the time, and if it wasn't burned, it was cooked badly. Eating that stuff would have been disrespectful to my mouth. I wasn't exactly a world traveler back then, and my appreciation of other cultures had yet to develop, so I wouldn't even try it. My solution was to eat a lot of vegetables and cheese sandwiches, and call it a day after that.

To make things even crazier, the Chernobyl disaster had happened on April 26, a couple of weeks before we flew out to Europe. The promoters weren't sure whether the dates would happen after that. They were really worried about the winds carrying radiation over to western Europe, where we had dates booked. They thought the food might be irradiated, in particular the vegetables, which was bad because, like I said, that was mostly what I ate when I was there. They even told us not to walk on the grass in case it was dangerous and gave you cancer. There were so many rumors flying around, and I felt very naive and very scared.

But it was still a lot of fun, because were on the road with the guys in Overkill and Agent Steel. All three bands and their crews were in a single, upright-seat bus, and you want to talk about ballbusting? Holy shit. I love Overkill, those guys are my long-time brothers, and although we didn't know Agent Steel, they were cool guys and we got on really well with them.

In the three bands, everybody had their little group of ballbusters, because everyone had different personalities. You could listen to each of these groups and it was like watching a comedy routine on TV. You'd start to laugh, and they'd see that and start laughing, too, and pretty soon everybody was fucking dying with laughter. That was literally our entertainment on that tour.

Sure, sometimes it got a little serious. If something went wrong for one of the bands during the show, that band would be screaming about it afterward. You learned really quickly whom you had to back off of, and whom you could go into. It was a great way to learn about people. You could see that a guy was slowly getting pissed off, and you knew if you started laughing at him, he'd go nuts. It was the best. There's always one sensitive guy who can't take it, which makes it even funnier.

A couple of weeks into that three-and-a-half-week tour, I started to get homesick. I missed the food at home. I'm serious about this—food is that important to me. I know it sounds silly. And it's not like alcohol made me feel better, either, because when it came to drinking, I still wasn't doing much of that. I mostly drank soda water. Pretty rock and roll, I know. The members of Anthrax generally didn't drink a lot until the nineties, when we started hanging out with Dimebag Darrell. Sure, I'd have a beer with Metallica when we toured with them, but for every three beers they drank, I'd drink one.

When we got home to America, thankfully having avoided the radiation we were so worried about, we did a couple of shows at L'Amour's, which was always a great venue for us because they paid great. Most years, we also played there around Christmastime, which was how we got money to buy gifts for everybody. It was a legendary place to play. Iron Maiden and Accept had played there before us.

The only downside of playing at L'Amour's was that the stereo would get stolen out of your car when you were inside. Seriously— you could rely on that happening. There was a crime ring that knew what time the rockers were going to be inside, so when the show started they smashed all the windows and took the car stereos.

It happened to me once. You come out of the club with a few beers in you, you see the broken window of your car and the hole where the stereo used to be, and you'd start yelling for blood and looking around to find the idiot who broke into your car. If you ever saw who did it, you would have kicked the shit out of him, but you never saw anyone because they were smarter than that. After a while you knew you were fucked, so you went and got a new stereo and a new window.

My next stereo was removable. Remember when you could get those car stereos that you could pull out with a handle, and carry around with you? Fuck you, stereo robbers.

Talking of getting into fights, it only ever happened twice to me as an adult. Once when we were playing at the Barrowland Ballroom in Glasgow, Scotland, in 1989, my friend Andy Buchanan was taking photos of us from the photo pit. He's a great buddy to Anthrax, a Scottish guy who can go toe-to-toe with any of us when it comes to ballbusting.

I was up onstage playing, and I looked over at Andy at one point, and it looked like he was having words with one of the bouncers. Next thing I know, they were on him, beating him up, so I threw down my bass and jumped right in. I only wanted to break it up, but then one of them hit me, and I saw red.

I never hit anyone unless I'm hit first, because I learned a long time ago never to take the first swing, but if I get hit, then I hit back. Immediately, it turned into a melee with fists everywhere. I think Scott got involved, too. It was pretty ugly. There's a video of it on YouTube somewhere.

The only other fight I can remember was in LA, again when we were playing, although it was more of a choke-out than a fight. This one security guy was supposed to protect the band, but he sees Joey Belladonna and he thinks Joey is a fan who got on our stage, right? So he takes Joey down and jumps on top of him. I see this, and I drop my bass and dive on top of the guy.

Before you know it, the crew dive in, too, and it's like one big sandwich of people. I wasn't hitting the security guy, I was just trying to get him to let go of Joey. Joey's not a big guy, and this huge, burly dude is crushing him. You literally couldn't see Joey under this giant motherfucker, and I thought our singer was going to be injured if I didn't rescue him, so I grabbed the guy by the neck and pulled him back. As I was doing this, I was thinking, *What the fuck am I doing? This isn't my job. I'm supposed to be playing bass!* Finally, they peeled me off, and it was cleared up, but it was pretty chaotic for a minute there.

Holy shit, these stories are crazy. You probably think I'm nuts, but hang on—it gets way crazier.

6
Cliff

AFTER PLAYING THOSE SHOWS at L'Amour's in the summer of 1986, we had about seven weeks before we were heading to Europe again, this time with Metallica. Uncle Joe said, "You want to work?" and there I was, back in the deli, cutting up liverwurst for that crazy old lady. It was pretty surreal, although I was happy to be home.

It got more surreal when we found ourselves mixing our third album, *Among the Living*, at Compass Point in Nassau in the Bahamas. What the fuck? Real rock stars mixed in the Bahamas, not people like us. Our heroes Iron Maiden had recorded there. Fortunately, the Island Records owner Chris Blackwell owned the studio, so we knew we'd get a good deal when we went down to mix the album there.

We recorded the album in Florida, which was also an amazing experience for us, because we were used to freezing our balls off all the time. So these were the great advantages of being in Anthrax, yet again. And when we got to Compass Point—which, let me say one more time, is in the fucking Bahamas!—we were over the moon. They gave us a great condo to live in, which had its own chef who cooked anything you wanted. All we had to do was listen to mixes all day. Not bad, huh?

There was this one sunny spot where we used to go and have a drink on a break from the mixing, and the beach was right there in front of us. It was just incredible. This was moving up in the world. It really felt as if Anthrax's fortunes had taken a leap.

Of course, all this luxury was coming out of our pockets. We were all savvy about that, but at the same time I wasn't worried about money. I knew I'd make a living somehow. I was too independent not to make it work if I had to. Nowadays, I wouldn't necessarily blow all that money on mixing in the Bahamas when it could easily be done in New York, but back then I wanted to experience that ride and enjoy the prestige of being in the company of people like Iron Maiden. I was curious to see what that lifestyle was like, and the answer is that it was a great experience that bonded us and felt like a pat on the back for working so hard. Everybody felt the vibe. It was a big deal for us.

When we recorded *Among* in Florida, our producer was Eddie Kramer, who had worked with a huge list of musicians, from Led Zeppelin and Kiss to the Rolling Stones and beyond. Eddie was very open to my ideas about bass, which was great because I really wanted to tap into his experience with all the great bands he'd worked with.

He was right there when we were engineering the tones for the bass. I kept experimenting with different sounds, and I kept saying no, although I didn't mean to be a pain. I kept saying, "I'll know when I hear it," and Eddie got a little frustrated after a while, but in the end we used a Marshall transistor head and some compression and eventually we got to the sound I was hearing in my head. Your sound and your playing are your personality, so no one can tell me what to sound like. It has to sound like me, or it won't be true.

The song "Caught in a Mosh" is probably the song where I'm most at front and center, because it has the bass intro that everyone knows, which Charlie wrote. At any Anthrax show, the moment when I start playing that riff is when the madness starts, because the crowd always goes nuts. We were recently asked by a Netflix series if they could use that song, and I love the fact that young metal fans are listening to it, thirty-five years after we recorded it, and getting into it.

I remember when we were at Compass Point—which I may or may not have mentioned is located in the Bahamas—there was this great little bar just down the road from the studio, where the band U2 had been hanging out. We walked in one day and the barman told us we just missed them, which crushed us because, believe it or not, Anthrax are the world's biggest U2 fans.

We met them a few years later, probably around 1990. It was backstage at Giants Stadium in Jersey, and our security guy knew U2, so he was able to get me and Charlie to meet them. We walked in and the first person we see is Bruce Springsteen over in the corner of the room. Then Bono comes over to talk to us.

He says, "Hi, guys. You know, The Edge has your records."

That blew our minds like you wouldn't believe. I thought, "I don't belong here—I'm just a metal guy!" but Bono and Larry and Edge made us feel so welcome. I ended up sitting on the couch with Adam Clayton and having a two-hour conversation with him about bass guitars, and what made it special was that he was genuinely interested in what I had to say. The whole night felt like a reward of some kind.

I wish I'd had the balls to say hello to Springsteen, though, because I'm such a fan. I've been in that situation since then, and I always try to overcome that sense of being starstruck and actually say hello. I remember being at the Grammys the last time we were nominated, and we were waiting in a holding pen before our category was announced. Paul McCartney was in the spot next to us, and Charlie and I said hello to him. I didn't try to shake his hand or anything or put that burden on him: just saying hello was enough. What was beautiful was that Paul made a point of saying hello to Charlie's daughter, who was also with us. What a nice guy.

Who else? Oh, yes, I went to see Lady Gaga. Let me tell you something—I really, really admire her, because I know where she came from. She's worked hard to be the success that she is. I went to one of her shows, and I went backstage, although I didn't know Gaga was there. When she saw me, she called my name out, like she knew me! Again, another person who's worked hard to get to the top, but who still has that human connection.

Another time, I was walking through Central Park. This was around 1996, and I'd gone into Manhattan for an acting audition. As I was walking along, I could see someone walking toward me, although I wasn't really focused on him because I was thinking about something else. After a minute it suddenly dawned on me that it was Sting.

"Holy shit!" I thought. "It's fucking Sting!" because I'm a huge Police fan.

By the time I realized who it was, and my brain had registered that it was a hero of mine, Sting had pretty much passed me. I would never normally do this, but this time I was determined to seize the moment, and as he passed I said, "Hey, Sting, my name is Frank Bello and I'm a big fan of your music."

Sting turned to look at me, and at first he was a little standoffish, which was understandable, but when I told him I played bass in a band named Anthrax he warmed up, because that had opened the door.

He said, "Come on, walk with me," so now it's Sting and Frank walking through Central Park, right? He told me he had writer's block and was trying to deal with it by walking in the park, close to where he lived in Manhattan. He says, "It baffles me. It just comes and it locks me up," and we talked about the Police and had a nice conversation about music. I didn't want to be a dick, so after fifteen minutes I left him in peace.

Well, if we're talking about celebrity encounters here, I have to mention the late Don Rickles. For anyone who doesn't know who Don was, he was Frank Sinatra's favorite comedian, and he would appear on *The Tonight Show Starring Johnny Carson* and tour the clubs, pulling people out of the audience and breaking their balls. He was famous for it. He would insult people right to their face, which looked brutal but was really funny.

My wife and I went to see Don perform in Long Island on our anniversary one year, and we had great seats in the second row. We were three feet from the stage. The show was in the round, and he was on the other side from us, making fun of somebody in the audience.

It was so funny that I suddenly laughed out loud, although it came out as this weird cackle. Don heard it and turned his head to look at me while continuing to insult this other person.

Oh, fuck! I ducked my head down, saying to my wife, "Shit. I think he saw me. Don't let him pick me out." Of course, what happens next? He comes right over and shouts, "You! Get up here!" at me, like a teacher yelling at a student in school.

I get up, and the seat in front of me is empty, so I climb over it to get to the stage, but like an asshole I fall over. He's shouting at me and everyone in our section is laughing, because I'm being such a buffoon. I was nervous as shit, and I'm never afraid to go on any stage—except this one.

I get up there, with some other poor guy that he pulled out of the audience, and he does a skit that I knew because I'd seen it before, where he's a Japanese army officer ordering us around. He kept dropping the mic and shouting "pick it up!" at us. The crowd's laughing their asses off.

Then Don says, "What's your name?" and I say, "Frank Bello." He instantly makes fun of me for being Italian. Then he says, "What do you do for a living?" and I say, "I'm a musician," but some guy at the back shouts, "He plays in a band called Anthrax!"

I was fucking mortified, but Don didn't hear it, thank God. He asked me, "What does your father do for a living?" and I said I didn't know. Then he said, "Whaddya mean, you don't know?" and continued to belittle me. It was the scariest time I've ever had onstage, but at the same time, one of the best.

These memories…I swear, I can't believe I lived through all this.

So, we're back in 1986, and we're about to go on tour in Europe with Metallica. Like I said, I knew them a bit, because every time they played New York before that, I'd go and see them and hang out backstage. The two bands had Jonny Z in common and we were coming up together. Jonny always put his bands together, which I thought was cool, so when we found out that we were going to Europe with Metallica, we were like, "Fuck yeah— let's go!" because—once again— it felt like another next step up. I'm a fan of both Metallica and Anthrax and I knew, as a fan, that this would be the show to see for the headbangers in Europe.

The first show was on September 10, and this time I wasn't so homesick, because we were on a mission now to get to the next level. Not only that—touring was now becoming an addiction. We wanted to get to the next stage and hit the road and play live in front of people, because that feeling is like a drug. You don't want to play one-off shows where you leave when you're done and you don't play for a month. You want to play on a consistent tour, which in those days was almost every night, and you know that's the way to get there.

We could feel a groundswell for our band: something was happening. Metallica had a great buzz going, too, and we wanted to be connected to that, so of course we were motivated because the roadmap was in front of us. For all those reasons, feeling homesick wasn't even in the picture anymore. Road life took over, and I couldn't wait to play and get that amazing feeling.

In fact, the only thing I disliked about those shows was that we got spit on constantly. I came home from that tour with so much DNA in my mouth from other people spitting in it. That happens because I have a deviated septum from having my nose busted in sports, and just from being clumsy, so my mouth is usually open when I play, and sometimes spit would land in it. The spotlight was right on me every night, and the loogies were coming at me, so I'd literally duck to avoid them.

I get it—back then, people supposedly did it because they loved us—but let me tell you, there is nothing worse than smelling your own hair after a couple of songs of being spit on. It smelled like someone else's bad breath. That was the worst part. My bass looked like it was covered in sweat after the show, but it wasn't sweat, it was fucking spit.

You probably think this is disgusting, and you're right, because it is. My mouth was open one day and a giant loogie flew in, right to the back of my throat, and I inhaled it. I immediately went to the side of the stage and threw up everything I'd eaten for a week. My tech was like, "What the fuck is going on?" but I didn't answer, because I couldn't speak. I went straight back onstage and started playing the next song.

Metallica got it even worse than we did. I vividly remember poor Cliff being right under a massive spotlight, right at the front of the stage, playing his wah pedal, and the air above him had so much spit flying through it that it looked like a cloud of hovering bugs. His jean jacket would be covered in gobs of spit when he came offstage.

You want to talk about paying dues? Sometimes there weren't showers after the gig, so you'd get in the sink and try to wash all the spit out with soap and water. Then you'd get into your bunk, which was just a wood panel because the tour buses were so bad back then, and then you'd pass out exhausted—and you'd wake up with your face in your own hair, which stank of spit. I still have that smell in my nose. You never lose it. Good times!

Nowadays, if somebody spit on me, I'd have them arrested. It's dangerous. We didn't think that way back then, I don't know why. We went with it. What were we gonna do, fight it?

Later on, we played tours with Motörhead and I saw Lemmy tell the crowds, "Spit one more fucking time and the show is over." Then someone would spit and, just like he promised, they walked offstage. He wasn't gonna tolerate that shit.

We all bonded with each other on that tour, even though it was cut short after two weeks for the very worst reason. I've always gotten along well with James Hetfield. He and Cliff were very close friends, and I would have drinks and laugh my ass off with them. We'd be talking about stupid shit and joking. Those are the times I still cherish. Nobody knew the future, but we were all on this journey together and we were so happy to be there.

James is always a great ballbuster. One night he, Lars Ulrich, and Kirk Hammett came to an Anthrax show in San Francisco, and I remember they were at the side of the stage. This was when John Bush was in the band, and James loves the song "Only" that Bush sang on, so he's rocking at the side with the rest of Metallica.

We went out afterward and I thanked him for coming along. He said, "Yeah, but I couldn't hear the bass." He started fucking with me, like, "Were you playing tonight? Was the bass plugged in?" and all this stuff. It was really funny. Whenever I hear a loud bass player now, I think of him.

The good times didn't last, unfortunately.

I vividly remember the morning of September 27, 1986. We were in the hotel lobby in Copenhagen. Our tour manager came up to us and he was all shaken up. He said, "Metallica's bus crashed last night, and Cliff was killed."

I said, "What? That can't be true. I spoke to him last night. This isn't real."

Of course, it was true, but it didn't compute to me. I was thinking, "That can't happen. It's Cliff. Maybe they just got the report wrong and he's just injured in the hospital." It was my first time dealing with death, ever in my life—someone that I saw every day, be taken away—and my brain refused to accept it.

The tour manager said, "No, it's real."

It just didn't make sense. Everything was rolling perfectly on that tour. We were two weeks in, so the camaraderie was there, and the whole thing was happening. I couldn't understand how he could be in a crash; I thought we had professional drivers taking care of us.

How the fuck could that happen?

It couldn't happen.

It *did* happen.

It was a stake in my heart, from that moment on—and it got progressively worse, from that moment on. Lars went home to his parents in Copenhagen, but James and Kirk showed up at the hotel that afternoon, and we were all hugging and crying and saying, "What the fuck? What the fuck?"

I've never felt sorrow from people as keenly as I felt it that night. James was broken, emotionally, and Charlie and I walked through the streets with him, trying to hold him up. We were just trying to talk him through it so he wouldn't be alone because he was so distraught. I was just trying to alleviate his pain in any way I could, so I was literally a shoulder for him to lean on as we walked through the city.

I've had some sad times in my life, but that was one of the saddest, walking through the streets with James.

The next morning, we woke up with a feeling of disbelief, and questions about what would happen next. Would the tour be canceled? Would we continue on ourselves? I didn't want to do that. Our friend just passed, and we needed to go home and get our shit together. It was a very hard time for us all, but especially for Metallica, who had lost a family member who was important to the writing, the vibe, and the inner workings of that band. I give them full credit for that, and we had a different level of compassion and closeness to Metallica after that night. I'm sure they felt it with us, too, because we were there.

No one really knows what caused Metallica's bus to crash, but one thing I can tell you is that tour buses were pretty dangerous back then. Nowadays, we have a comfortable, professional tour bus, but back then nobody trusted those fucking buses. The one we used on that tour was a regular bus that used to have seats. They just took the seats out and replaced them with thin wood on the side of the bunks, up against the windows.

Maybe it wasn't even wood—it looked like cardboard to me. It was very thin against the window, and you could feel how dangerous it was when you were lying in the bunk. If there was just a little scratch carved out of the wood, you could see through it and out of the window. That's how thin it was.

In hindsight, it all makes sense. How unsafe were those fucking buses? Who knows what the fuck happened. It was just a horrible, horrible circumstance to be in.

What drives me crazy is that we've been cheated of so much more music from Cliff. He had a whole lot more amazing, innovative art in him. Think how young he was when he died, and how great he was even at that young age. He was way beyond everybody else, and so far ahead of the game that I can't even imagine what he'd be doing right now. I still love him and his music to this day.

An important member of the metal community passed away that day. I looked up to Cliff and I admired what he did, because he was an innovator. And now he was gone, and that was a big deal, for Metallica's music and for us all in this movement.

I used to go to Metallica's soundboard, next to their sound guy Big Mick, and watch the show from there. Cliff would do something different in his solo every night. The way he used that wah pedal was completely innovative. He was the foundation of that band, as I saw it.

After every show the two bands would have dinner together. Cliff and I would talk bass and have some laughs, because he was such a funny guy. He and I always said this stupid thing to each other when we left the venue: one of us would say, "Maybe I'll see you later," and the other one would answer, "Maybe I will." It was just a funny little thing that we said to each other every night, as a stupid joke that made us laugh.

My very last memory of Cliff is still totally vivid. I said, "Maybe I'll see you later," and his last words to me as he was walking out of the building, looking back at me, were, "Maybe I will." I can still see his face as he said it. That's my last memory of him.

The remaining month of tour dates was canceled. It was really disappointing, on top of the shock and sadness of Cliff's death, because we knew the tour was going to take us to the next level.

Live your life. Every moment, every second that you have—*live it*.

7
Who's the Man?

YOU GO THROUGH CHALLENGES and trials in life, and you may succeed or you may fail when they come your way, but in both cases you come out stronger—and that was the way my life was going in 1987. After the shock of Cliff Burton's death, I did what I always did and retreated to my grandmother's house. That was an oasis for me once again: the place where I was protected from all the harms of life.

My hours at the deli were cut because Joe needed somebody who would always be there, and I was going to be on tour all the time from 1987 onward. I still worked weekends when I was home, though, and it was a healing experience for me after the trauma of the European tour.

In July '87, I was twenty-two years old and gaining confidence. Our album, *Among the Living*, was out, and it was a mature piece of work that has stood the test of time. As a bass player, I knew I'd done a good job. My style was developing from one influenced by my heroes into my own way of playing. That definitely came out on the new album, and I was very happy about that because I knew what to do with the songs as we wrote them. I thought to myself, "What can I do on the bass to enhance this tasty part here and this tasty part there?"

Without meaning to bore you about bass playing, I need to explain that the tone of my parts was a challenge, too. If you listen to *Spreading the Disease*, for example, the bass tone is less audible because I was scared and just wanted a standard tone. My playing reflected my personality on that record, and I was young and nervous, so it doesn't stand out—but when we came to record *Among the Living*, I was working with a production legend, Eddie Kramer, and I also felt much more comfortable in my skin as a bass player.

The challenge with *Among* was that Scott's thick guitar sound and Charlie's kick drums made it difficult for me to be heard at the low end, and believe me, Eddie and I tried a lot of different tones. We knew the bass needed to cut through, so we needed to find a frequency that was right in the middle of the drums and guitars, and we found it after a lot of experimenting. Eddie was a great producer. He gave me a chance to be heard, and not just in terms of volume, which was very satisfying.

I guess what I was doing at this point was synthesizing everything I'd learned as a bass player. A lot of people have been kind enough to compliment me on my playing over the years: that started around the time of *Among* because the tone we found made the bass audible, and also because I'd gained confidence, like I said.

When people ask me to talk about my influences, I should really start with Paul McCartney, who has been such an inspiration to me over the years, and I haven't ever really thought about it. Talk about a guy who is not just a songwriter but who added so much to the songs with his bass lines. He has a beautiful voice as well, and the bass adds so much melody to the songs. Listen to "Penny Lane," where he plays a descending line in one verse and then plays it again—but an octave lower—in the next verse. And we're still talking about it all these years later.

Like I said earlier, I grew up listening to Cheap Trick, and specifically their bass player Tom Petersson. He's a great bassist and very underrated. It was his tone that got me, from his 8-string and 12-string basses. The lines weren't complicated, but I don't think they needed to be, because that piano-like tone—which came from three octaves of strings, because of the little piccolo strings—just blew my mind. How he got the right amp for that tone, I have no idea.

Now let's talk Geezer Butler. I know the whole Ozzy period was amazing, but I love the Dio era, too. There are so many great bass parts on the *Heaven and Hell* album, right from the first song, "Neon Knights." Geezer is having so much fun in that song. Not only are the songs great, but the bass parts are amazing, too. Listen to the song "Heaven and Hell": Geezer is telling a story within a story, just with the bass part. When you can sing a bass line like that one, how much of a compliment is that?

You know by now that Geddy Lee is one of my biggest influences. The intricacy of his scales and the synching-up with the drums really add up to a celebration of the bass. That whole approach is so inspiring to me to this day, and when I listen to a song like "YYZ," I have to pick up my bass and play along. The bass is meant to be played like that, and I just have to follow it. Synching the bass and drums like Rush used to do is not a thought process: it's just a natural talent. I was just listening to it the other day and it's beautiful.

Of course, every song Steve Harris does is like a bass exercise, but fun. That's how Steve writes. I've gotten to know him over the years and I've asked him lots of questions about how he did it. He's one of my favorite bass players in the world, and he still has the fire.

•••

We had a full year ahead. We were going to release "I Am the Law," Scott's song about Judge Dredd, as a single, with a goofy rap song on the B-side called "I'm the Man." We were going on tour with Metallica again in Europe, we were going to play the fabled Monsters of Rock at Donington in England, and we were going to tour America with Testament. Looking back from today's point of view, does it get any more metal than that?

When we went out with Metallica again, we got to know Cliff's replacement, Jason Newsted. He was a good guy and came up to me to say that he liked my bass playing. He did a great job on that tour, even though he was trying to fill shoes that were impossible to fill.

The Metallica guys put him through the mill, too. We used to go out with them after the shows and drink up a storm at the hotel bars, although I was still a lightweight and had to call it a night after three or four beers. If they introduced whiskey shots, I'd throw up. Jason always got stuck with the bar tab, but he'd laugh it off like a trooper, even though whatever money he was making, it was going on those bills. I felt for him, but I guess it was part of the gig: whoever got that spot in Metallica was going to get it.

I started making a decent salary after *Among the Living*. Like I said, there had been no money around the *Spreading the Disease* album, even though we were signed to a major label. Thank God I could still go home after whatever sporadic tours we did and work in Joe's Deli. After *Among the Living*, we were on the road a lot; we almost never came home. The money got bigger, the advances got bigger, and all the good stuff started coming in because we were busting our fucking asses.

What's funny is that Charlie and I would come home from tour, but we were both still living at my grandmother's house, so we would get a taxi from the airport, walk in with our suitcases, and just go to our rooms. Then we'd see each other at the dinner table a couple of hours later and say, "Hey." Even after a long tour, we were still together.

That takes a lot of heart. Think about it. We were never away from each other in Anthrax, especially in those early days. I had my group of friends back home in the Bronx, but the guys in the band were both my friends and my family, love them or hate them, and there's some of both in our band, just like there is in any family.

We stuck with each other, though. I regard Anthrax's career as a series of peaks and valleys. The year 1987 was a peak, and we stayed up there through *State of Euphoria* and *Persistence of Time* until 1991 or '92, when grunge came up and the *Sound of White Noise* album had to compete against it. We had a new singer, too, so it was a perfect storm. All that is coming up, so stay tuned.

On August 22, 1987, we played Monsters of Rock in England. Bon Jovi was headlining and Cinderella opened the show. Then it was WASP, us, Metallica, and Dio. It was surreal, because we were on the rise and everybody was there. Not only was the show great, but the audience was incredible. It was a big high for Anthrax.

I have a crazy story from that show involving a particular rock star: you can probably figure out who it was. Right before we go onstage, I go to take a piss in the toilets' cabin, because I always do that right before Anthrax plays. I'm standing there, in mid-stream, and nobody else is in there. Suddenly this giant hand lands on my shoulder and starts tapping me.

"You gotta go."

I look up, and this enormous man is standing next to me.

"I'm in mid-stream here, but I'm going onstage in a minute," I tell him, thinking, "Fuck this guy!" to myself.

"No. You gotta go right now," he snarls. "The man's gotta go."

I didn't know what he was talking about. What man? Who is "the man"? And what's more, when you're peeing and you start talking to somebody, you stop peeing, right? So now I have even more pissing to do, and now I'm feeling the pressure because we're literally one minute away from stage time.

Now I'm starting to get a little heated. "Dude, I'm fucking pissing here!"

He repeats, "The man's gotta go. You gotta go now!" He's getting mad.

I say, "I don't know what the fuck you're talking about, but I ain't moving!" and I turn my back on him. But now I'm feeling the pressure of someone looking at me and I can't pee. Finally, I squeeze out a few drops and leave.

Outside, I swear to God it's the famous rock star, standing right there, glaring at me. He needs to take a shit, but they had to clear the bathroom first. Why? I have no idea. He had his security kick me out before he went in there. Why didn't he have his own bathroom? I couldn't listen to that band ever again after that.

On the other hand, Ronnie James Dio was there. Now, Ronnie was one of the best people on this Earth. He was a New York guy with a God-given voice, and I completely related to him, because he was such a beautiful person. I met him a lot over the years at shows, and told him I was a fan, and got to know him. He was a legend, and I respected him for his sheer greatness. Joey was close to him, too; they bonded because they were both singers and both upstate New York guys. It was great to see those two amazing singers talking shop.

The last time I talked to Ronnie, Anthrax was supporting Heaven and Hell in Greece in July 2009. We were in a bar at the top of our hotel where everybody hung out. There was a view of the Acropolis, and the vibe was great. It was my birthday that day and Ronnie's the next day, and we were both die-hard Yankees fans so we would always talk about the games. That night we weren't talking metal, we were just two New York guys talking baseball. He knew it was my birthday, so he goes to the bartender, "Can I have two beers?" It was just me and Ronnie James Dio, celebrating our birthdays.

Come on, man. Nothing gets better than that, and I'll cherish that experience until the day I die.

Around that time, we released a video called *Oidivnikufesin*, recorded at the Hammersmith Odeon in London, England. I gave copies to my family, and it's a sign of my mom and grandmother's love for me that they watched it and enjoyed it, even though Anthrax didn't play music that they necessarily enjoyed. They were just happy to see me and Charlie doing well in life. That's the sign of a loving family. They couldn't have been more supportive about me pursuing my calling, and they worked hard to give me that freedom.

What's funny is that I didn't really enjoy *Oidivnikufesin* because I have a really hard time watching myself on screen. I'm so critical of everything I do. I always say, "Man, I should've done something different here." When I see myself in interviews, I'm like, "What the fuck did you say? And what's that New York accent?" In Anthrax videos, too, and even in songs—I listen to myself and I think, "I should have done this," or, "I should have done that."

When I see myself onstage with Anthrax, I am so critical of myself. I think, "What are you doing there? You look ridiculous." If I do a jump off the drum riser, I think, "What the fuck? That wasn't a good jump." Maybe it's because I'm a perfectionist. I know I'll never get it exactly the way I want it, but I'll always give it my best shot.

We were going places now, after all that work. I attribute a lot of that to that great spirit of my brothers in this band. The great thing about being in Anthrax is having such long-time fans. As we get older, the metal community knows how lucky we are to have this music to follow. The payback is so great. The way it makes us feel enables us to get through life. It's taken me through really hard times at different parts of my life, and thankfully it's always been there to hold my hand.

As I'm sure you've grasped by now, music is a therapy for me. It helps me through life, and it gives me mental stability and security. It allows me to go to the next stage of life. I won't be stable enough to enjoy relationships with friends without music. It's all one.

I wish more people would understand the importance of music—literally, how to *be* with music. It feeds your soul, which is why, when I see my son Brandon enjoy music the way he does, I can see that it's more than just enjoyment for him. He's getting his angst out by listening to crazy, heavy music, and it's helping him therapeutically through the tough times. I want him to have that tool for living.

Then there's playing with a band. There is nothing more satisfying and fulfilling and warming than picking up a guitar or a bass and playing through a song and making sense of it. When I was young, that felt like a great accomplishment and it made me feel that I was one with the music. I still do that: I'll pick up an acoustic or electric guitar and write a song and sing it.

Putting a song out that you created is so satisfying, even though you might just be singing to a wall. That's my magic. Take that into a band and there is literally nothing more fulfilling, because you're sharing it and feeding that energy to the audience, who then feeds it back to you. We both understand why we're there.

People think we're playing to the audience: no, we're playing *for* the audience, and the audience is giving it right back, creating a great big high together. It's a feedback loop that bounces right back, and that energy can't be touched. When I see someone go nuts when we start to play a song that they love, that's me out there—I'm living through them. That's why I'm so energetic onstage, because I'm a fan who is lucky enough to play this stuff and make people feel like that. I want to get into it just as much as they are. I want to be part of it.

The music has always been there, the fans have always been there, and the camaraderie of metal has always been there. I'll never forget that. On my deathbed, I'll say, "That was a good fucking run." I'm very thankful. We have a uniform that we wear, there's a vibe and a hunger and an energy and this angst. Whatever walk of life you're from, this angst is met and soothed with this music and this community.

There's also a nurturing in this music, and perhaps men who are into metal don't like to use the word "nurturing" because it's so associated with femininity, but metal feeds us and satisfies the yearning that we have in our guts. It gives me a pathway through the puzzle of life. It makes the journey easier; it's my companion through life. And thank God for this companion.

I'll go even further, if you'll permit me, and talk about the nurturing that I received from my grandmother Tina. When she left the Earth in 2012, a lot of good things left with her. That's the truth. She died of lung cancer, although she never smoked a cigarette in her life. God rest her soul. I'm lucky to have had her in my life for so long; a lot of people don't have their grandparents around for so many years. She said to me, "I consider you more as a son than a grandson," which was a great compliment, and I miss her for that; no disrespect to my mother, whom I love dearly.

As I'm talking to you now, I'm thinking about wheeling Tina to her radiation treatment. In that situation, when you know what she's up against, you try to make the moment light. You try to take any way out of where you're actually going, which was a booth that she had to sit in and receive the radiation for her cancer, so I would say any stupid thing in my mind to make her laugh. I always have a lot of stupid things in my mind, so that was easy for me.

She never drank or smoked in her life, but I'd say, "C'mon, Tina, get in the wheelchair. We'll stop off at the store and I'll get you some booze and cigarettes." That would make her laugh and say, "Shut up!" because she knew exactly why I was doing it. When she was having the radiation, I'd wait in the waiting room and I'd pick her up in the wheelchair when she was done and go right back to the car and drive her home.

Those times were among the closest I've ever felt to her, but at the same time those were some of the most painful times. It was stage IV cancer, so she knew it was inevitable, and we all knew it, too. I hated it when I heard her cough, because she never coughed like that before. I still have those coughs in my mind; it's all very real to me. My wife Teresa also loved her; they were very close.

Later, I wrote a song called "Booze and Cigarettes" about that with Altitudes & Attitude, my band with David Ellefson of Megadeth. People might think it's just about drinking and smoking and partying, but of course it's not.

Charlie and I were on tour with Anthrax as my grandmother was passing, and it was such a tough time for the band. We've never had a harder time, Charlie and I. It reveals the greatness of the people in Anthrax, and the brotherhood and love within the band, and why we've stayed a band for so long. Joey, Scott, and Rob Caggiano knew what we were going through, and that both of us had to go home to say goodbye. I appreciate the people in Anthrax, because were able to do that without canceling everything, and I have to thank the fans. I also appreciate my friend and manager Mike Monterulo, who went above and beyond for me at this terrible time.

I remember the time when I had to go and say goodbye to my grandmother. I knew exactly what was going to happen. You have that vision of the hospital bed, and all that. I knew Charlie was home already, and I really didn't want to face him, because I knew it was his mom. It was like looking at your brother, acknowledging that our mom, or our grandmother, is passing, and we have to send her off and move on.

Somehow we had to pick up the pieces and move on from this—and go back on tour. You just try to take what they taught you and utilize it in the most positive way. To this day, when factions of my family fight, I'll try and resolve it in her name. Tina would talk to both sides and be the mediator, and I've recently done the same thing. I said, "This is ridiculous. Tina would never let this happen. You guys both need to grow up."

Metal fans are all heart. They understood exactly what we were going through, because they're smart and they were in touch with us emotionally. They're very intelligent people, and they often don't get credit for that, but they really are. They completely understood when Joey announced onstage that Charlie wasn't there that night.

Fans would say to me, "I'm sorry to hear about your grandmother." They got it. The fans feel like an extension of us and of our family, which is why I feel so close to them. They're good, genuine people, and I think metal has lasted so long because of the people. We're all one. We're the guys onstage doing the entertaining, I get that, but we're all one because I want to get you crazy the way you want to get me crazy. We feed off each other. That's how it's always been, and I don't want it to ever change.

Thanks for letting me talk about Tina for a while there. It's important to me that you understand what she meant to me and Charlie—and what I learned from her is totally connected to the life lessons that I want to pass on in this book.

8

Euphoric Persistence

IN EARLY 1988, ANTHRAX was truly on a roll. We were writing and recording our next album, *State of Euphoria*, and we had tour on top of tour on top of tour booked ahead of us. That's a huge compliment right there, because it means that a lot of people—maybe hundreds of thousands—want to see you play. The downside is that you're never home and you never see your loved ones, but it's still a great problem to have. You're on your way up, so you don't want to screw up.

State of Euphoria isn't a bad record, but maybe it wasn't up to our usual high standards. I think that was the one time in Anthrax when the business got in the way of the art. The way we usually work is that we make all our albums completely perfect, or as perfect as they can possibly be, at least. They have to be exactly right, and on that album we didn't bake the cake until it was done, which is the best analogy I have. We needed to live with those songs just a little bit longer, and it would have been that much better.

I'm happy with the bass parts, it's the writing that could have been better. The song "Schism," for example—I would have done something different to the chorus. We should have examined it a little more. That song really irks me for that reason.

Still, what the fuck. I don't regret anything I've done, because it got me here, wherever I am. In fact, I don't believe in regrets at all, ever…even though our dress sense was a little vivid around this time.

Look at any picture of Anthrax from around this time, with the skateboard shirts and shorts and all that crazy stuff. You might think we looked like idiots, but let me tell you, I wore those shorts specifically for comfort. None of us fucking cared what people thought about the way we looked. Everybody has a youth and everybody deserves to have a great time while they're young.

"I don't want my balls sticking to my leg!"

That was always the line that I used when people asked me why we dressed that way, because the clothes became this big thing in people's minds.

Okay, we started wearing some crazy colors, and maybe I was a little out of line with those, for sure. I see photos of some of them and I think, "What the fuck were you thinking, Frank?" but then I remember that it was just a youthful thing that we did on the ride up. Why would I think negatively about it now when it was such a positive thing at the time? People started wearing the shorts at our shows, so it was an honest thing that came out of an attitude that said, "We don't give a fuck. We're gonna wear shorts!" Later on, quite honestly, I just felt like looking like Lemmy again and wearing pants. There's no rhyme or reason for it.

Business was getting very serious, not that our fans would ever know that from looking at us. Michael Mitnick, a New Yorker through and through who now lives in Florida, was our accountant for years: he's been a father figure to me for over twenty years now. He'll beat me down to a pulp when I'm out of line, figuratively speaking. When Anthrax got successful in the late eighties, he was our business manager, and I would go down to his office to do my taxes.

Michael and I got along really well. Because Anthrax was on tour all year, he would tell me how to adapt my spending habits on the road. I'm not a big spender, but he'd remind me to collect all my receipts so we could deduct touring expenses against taxes, as any well-run business has to do. Of course, when I came home, I'd give him a whole pile of mixed-up receipts to decipher, and he'd say, "What the hell is this?" and laugh at how disorganized I was. I'm much better at that these days, of course.

This was what was so great about Michael. We'd go out to lunch, and he'd ask me, "What comes after Anthrax, Frank?" He was always on me about that, and it scared the shit out of me because it was such a good question. I still don't know the answer. That question still fuels a fire under my ass to work hard, although I know there will always be opportunities no matter what happens. The way I look at life, I'll always make it somewhere else.

There's a lesson here for anyone who is looking after a family. Part of being a responsible person who wants to provide for their loved ones is facing up to these very difficult questions. They're challenging, and hard to answer, but you need to face up to them to do your job as a mother or a father. Look yourself in the mirror and ask, "What do I do if it all goes wrong?"

Of course, in 1988 I was almost never at home, and I rarely if ever took that question seriously, because Anthrax looked like it was going on forever. If I had two or three weeks at home, that was rare. When I say I was never home, I really mean it. I bought a condo a few years later, but I only used it to store all the stupid stuff I brought home from each tour. I'd literally throw my crap in there and go back out. It was a condo that I basically used as a storage locker.

So touring was a way of life for us now, and we had it set up so it was always one big party when we went out, largely because we always chose our friends to be our crew. They were our family away from our other family.

We had a lot of stupid fun on these tours. If we'd had camera phones back then, you would be so entertained to see all the crazy things we did. We didn't trash hotels to the extent of breaking down walls or anything, but we were on tour so long that we had to find ways to entertain ourselves, and those ways were often pretty wild.

One popular activity was targeting a member of our band or crew and playing terrible pranks on them. We called them Pirate Attacks and we would plan them out a long time in advance, because we were such evil fuckers. We'd get that day's victim's hotel room key—sometimes it might even be a magazine interviewer who was on the road with us—and we'd throw flour, eggs, and buckets of ice-cold water on them. We'd fill big fucking garbage cans with ice cubes, fill them up with water, run into the victim's room, and let them have it.

One of the crew guys would be on his bed, fucking a girl that he'd met, and we'd slam open the door, shout "Pirate Attack!" and, in the pitch dark, throw all this water and flour and eggs onto the loving couple. It was completely nuts. Insanity. Then we'd pick up the bed, with them on it, and flip it over before running back to our rooms, laughing our fucking asses off while he shouted, "What the fuck! What the fuck!"

Nobody ever locked their room, so it was easy to get in there and mess with people. They got me one time, but after that I learned to lock my door. I was smart about it, because I could see people exchanging looks during the day, so I knew they were planning to get me that night—and my door stayed locked, believe me.

It got worse. This one time, one of our crew guys took the biggest shit I've ever seen in my life. The end of it came out of the toilet bowl, it was so big. I swear it was a foot long. He got a

Pizza Hut box and scooped the fucking thing out. It looked like a huge, brown banana. I'm not exaggerating here—it was literally a foot long. It stank, of course, and it got used in a Pirate Attack on someone's room, which was horrible.

We toured with Living Colour that year, which was a blast because I'm big friends with those guys. They're such a great fucking band. They're family to me. The singer Corey Glover and I are very close. Scott and I played cameo roles in the video of their song "Open Letter (To a Landlord)," which was a huge honor.

Corey and I are great ballbusters to each other. I always remember, every night I'd watch their set, and I would make fun of Corey when they came offstage because he always hammed up the first line of this one song, like an opera singer. After a while this got into his head, and he'd look over at me as he did that line—and then ham it up hugely, watching me laugh my fucking ass off. We'd be crying with laughter afterward.

Kings X were on tour with us, too, and their singer Dug Pinnick and I had a mutual love of Cheap Trick's bassist Tom Petersson, who plays a 12-string bass, which sounds like a piano note on top of a bass note. This was such a good time, hanging out with these great people. They're our brothers and we love them forever.

I was single again in the late eighties, and I had a great time dating a lot of girls, although I wasn't a huge stud or anything. It wasn't about using my status as a rock musician to get girls' attention, either—I was just being a young guy and having fun. I would go out to LA and meet Scott, and we'd write songs and then go out and hang out with friends in Huntington Beach and Hollywood.

One of those guys was an actor, and I used to go up to Hollywood to see him and hang out. Let me tell you something—those were crazy, crazy nights. I never did drugs, but there was a lot of drinking, and a whole lot of women. My friend was pretty well-known in Hollywood circles, so any high-end club we wanted to get into, the entourage was right there. He was good with the girls, and like I said, I did pretty well myself. It was a fun time, and pretty much the only period of my life when I indulged in that kind of behavior. Being married is better, and much less exhausting.

The tours went on. We did the Headbangers Ball Tour with Exodus and Helloween, and we finished off the year by opening for Ozzy Osbourne. That tour was great. Ozzy's guitarist Zakk Wylde was from New Jersey, so he and I were friendly from day one. With that guy, it might be years since you saw him, but when you start talking it's like it was yesterday. I remember seeing him playing the guitar in the dressing room, and I couldn't believe what I was seeing. He was fucking ripping.

The whole band was great to us. Mike Inez, who was Ozzy's bass player back then and is now back in Alice in Chains, is one of the nicest people on the Earth. As for Ozzy, you could talk to him, but you had no idea where the conversation was going. He would ramble some stuff and then suddenly leave. He is a nice guy, though, and obviously a legend.

We were playing with Ozzy on New Year's Eve, and we stayed in the infamous Hyatt House hotel in Hollywood, which was very scary. It was like the movie *Rock Star*—which, by the way, they asked me to come out and audition for, because there was a part for a bass player, but I was on the East Coast so it didn't work out. There was serious rock 'n' roll history in that hotel, with Led Zeppelin and the rest of them—you can Google that—so we really let it all roll, with people running through the hallways and all that.

Security was pissed at us and kept coming up to our floor to yell at us, so every time we heard the elevator arrive, we just closed our doors and turned the music off. Those guys got so tired of us, but when we were on, we were fully on, and that was fucking party night.

Like I said, Scott and I were writing music out in LA, although you can interpret that loosely. It was more like hanging out, writing melodies, and seeing my actor friends. During the days, we would go out to a park near my friend Donovan's house and play a pickup game of basketball—and the coolest thing was that we often played with the Beastie Boys, who were his friends. We were huge Beastie Boys fans, but we didn't let on.

It was very intense, because these guys were good; I was a pretty decent ball player myself back then, so it was game on. We used to have these full-court games and they were very serious. Everybody got into it, but it was a fun time because we didn't talk business, we just played and then went our separate ways.

The new songs were for the next album, *Persistence of Time*, which came out in summer 1990. As this is my autobiography, I guess we should talk about our cover of Joe Jackson's "Got the Time," which has my bass intro and also a bass solo in the midsection. Charlie said, "Why don't we jam that song?" and we all lit up because we were all Joe Jackson fans.

I was like "Fuck yeah!" but not because there's a bass solo in that song. I'm not a bass solo guy. I just like to play the tasty bass lines, and I don't need a spotlight for my playing. They insisted, though, so I said, "Fine." The majority vote always wins in the democracy of Anthrax. It was a challenge because I wanted to make the solo simple and not overdo it. I love the original bass part by Graham Maby, but I didn't want to copy him because he's so clever and I wanted it to be a tribute to him.

I'd never really done a solo outside of my bedroom, so we took it apart piece by piece, asking what was going to work. I remember our producer Mark Dodson kept saying, "What do you got?

What do you got?" and I just kept making more stuff up on the spot and seeing what sounded good. I remember he wanted me to slap the bass, and I said, "Really?" and did that for him. I still love playing that song and seeing the crowd's reaction, right from the start. It's like "Caught in a Mosh" in that sense.

Life went on in the way it always does, with ups and downs. Actually, it was pretty much all ups, and the only down was when there was a fire at our practice space. I got a call one morning, saying, "Get over here! There's a fire!" Charlie and I lived ten minutes away from our studio, so we ran over there. I didn't know what kind of fire it was, or if it was a big fire or what, so I was shocked when I showed up and saw all these fucking flames. I thought it had been contained, but it wasn't, and all our shit was gone.

They told us it had been caused by something electrical, but they really weren't sure. Maybe some electric appliance was left on and got hot. It couldn't have been left on by us, so it must have been someone else, because there were other people using the place.

We all lost gear. I remember seeing Scott's prize amps, that we used for every fucking record, all melted. I kept seeing them pulling burned-up bass equipment out of there and thinking, "Shit. Not that!" Some classic amps that I had, including this old Sunn head that I used to love because it gave me that great Gene Simmons kind of fuzz, had melted away. That bummed me out. To add to the misery, some great Fender basses were actually stolen from the scene because I never recovered them. I couldn't get them myself because the fire teams wouldn't give us permission to go in.

This was another lesson in money management, I guess, and by this stage in our careers we were starting to understand how our business really worked. Generally, I don't think people understand how wealth accumulates in this industry, but that's nobody's fault:

why should anyone know the inner workings of the industry when they're outside it?

The truth is that you can have gold albums, and people will think you lead the life of a rich rock star, but it's not really like that. There's no millions of dollars going anywhere. A gold record is just for show—which can be cool, by the way; *Persistence of Time* went gold and we all got gold records—but you have to make a living.

How do we make a living? By touring. Okay. How do we tour?

The first thing to remember is that tours cost a lot of fucking money to set up—a hell of a lot. First of all, you have to get us all over to the country where we're booked to play, so you have to pay for flights and hotels for the band and the crew. All that is money that you pay up front. Here's the kicker: once all that is paid and the band is physically there and playing shows, the only real way to make money *is to stay on tour*. Literally, stay out there.

In Anthrax, we can't do a three-week tour and expect to make money. We start making money after three weeks because that's when we've recouped all the initial expenses. At that point you start making enough money to pay everyone, and the next step is to start putting money toward the next tour. The net result is that you never really pull any big sums of money out of the business.

You take a salary, of course, and it's a good salary in Anthrax's case, thank God. We're very fortunate because it's a fun way to make a living, although the downside of it is that you miss your family, and you miss your children growing up. And as you get older, touring gets harder, because you demand certain things. For example, I'm not going to tour in a van at my age, after all these years of work. I've been through the mill and paid my dues. Maybe if I was going to start a band on the side I'd go in a van, but not with Anthrax.

Even then, people say, "But you're playing these huge venues," which is true if you're a headline act of a certain level of popularity, but if you're an opening band you're not getting paid a lot. You'll get a fair deal, or better than a fair deal in some cases, but nobody's making hundreds of thousands of dollars opening for anybody. That's just the way it works. You're not doing that opening slot for the money, you're doing it in the hope of turning a bunch of the headline act's fans into Anthrax fans.

As the tours passed, we got savvy about this stuff. In the early days, we'd look at the income side of a spreadsheet and think, "Wow, we're making good money on this tour," and then we'd see the outgoings column and shit our pants, asking, "What the fuck happened to all that money?" We weren't that naive anymore.

That said, we came close to major financial problems when we toured with Iron Maiden in '88 because it was canceled after our flights and other expenses were paid for up front. We couldn't get a refund and we were facing a complete loss. Fortunately, Iron Maiden saved our asses and took care of a major debt that we were faced with.

Scott wrote about it in detail in his first book—and by the way, both of his books are awesome, so please read them if you haven't already. My lesson from that episode was how great Iron Maiden are. I want everyone to know that. Family takes care of family, and Iron Maiden have always been family. A true class act.

From what I just wrote, you might think that touring is a strange way to try and make a living. It's hard work, for sure, but it's also an absolute blast if you're prepared to accept that you'll meet some unbalanced people while you're out there. I remember one time we played Irvine Meadows in California, and a guy in the audience was throwing firecrackers at us. Now that's an assault. He put all of us in danger, as well as the entire audience. Why would you want to hurt people like that? You could put someone's eye out.

I remember jumping on this guy and getting into it with him. The way I grew up, if you put me or my band in danger, it's over. I don't want to fight, but if you threaten me, the gloves come off and I'm gonna pull your esophagus out...at least, that's what I'm thinking. Especially back in those days, which was long before today's relaxed, friendly, yoga- and meditation-loving Frank!

9

Acting Up

IN THE FALL OF 1989, I went to a nightclub in New Rochelle called Streets, and I was introduced to a beautiful woman called Teresa by our mutual friend, Fran. As soon as I saw her, I was blown away. I said hello to her, and we talked for hours. I knew that I wanted to be with her, right from that moment. I knew it was real.

I went on tour for quite a while after that, but we stayed in touch. Our first date didn't happen until September 1990, right when the movie *Goodfellas* was released. I'm a huge Martin Scorsese fan, as you'll have guessed because I keep referencing him in this book, and I couldn't wait to see that film.

I didn't care what else I was doing on the day it came out—I was going to see it. Teresa knew I was dying to see it, so we got advance tickets, went out in Secaucus, New Jersey, had dinner at an Italian restaurant right next to the cinema, and then saw the movie. That was our first official date.

We were inseparable from then on. Remember, there was no email or FaceTime back then, so when I was away on tour, Teresa and I used to call and write letters to each other, just talking about life and what we were doing. I remember when Anthrax was touring in Japan, I spent a lot of money on phone calls to Teresa because I needed to be in contact with her. She was my safe home.

When we got serious about our relationship, we sat down and talked about how it would work, with me away from home as much as I am. Everything was explained and agreed up front, and we began our committed relationship. I told her, "I'm going to be your boyfriend, and you can trust me. I won't be going with anybody else."

I brought Teresa out on tour in the early days. It was great to be with her, but touring wasn't for her. You have to understand, when you're on tour you're in and out of cities pretty fast. It's great if you're in the band, because you're doing press and sound checking and everything, but for everybody else, it's terrible—you don't get enough sleep, and the food is usually awful, and you never get a chance to see a city for longer than a few hours. So she came on the bus a couple of times, but after that, she had no intention of ever coming on tour again. I totally get that.

Teresa and I had a lot of great times with our extended families when I was home. We used to go over to Atlantic City and meet up in hotels and have a ball—eating great food, gambling in the casino, going to the beach. We'd do that for entire weekends, and we always had a wonderful time.

So here I am, in 1991—going steady and loving life. Let's keep going. There's a lot to talk about!

You know I've always been a fan of hip-hop because we talked about the Beastie Boys a few pages back—so when we recorded and toured with Public Enemy, that was huge for me. It was Scott who originally got me into that band. Charlie was into them, too. Their music was fucking heavy, even though it didn't have guitars until we brought them into it. You can find a certain weight and impact in any good music, if you're looking for it.

So when I heard that we were going to record the Public Enemy song "Bring the Noise" and have them guest on it, it all made sense because of who we are. One thing I've always loved about Anthrax is that we don't care where music comes from. All music should be as one: work on it, write songs, and see what comes out.

People say that we broke down barriers with that song, and that makes me happy. Nobody should be telling you how you should live your life. Break down the fucking barriers if you can because life is so fucking short. I celebrate Anthrax all the time for that reason. This is where we're going, and if you don't like it, don't listen to it.

The tour with Public Enemy was awesome from day one. The promoters were afraid, like, "We don't know what's going to happen, with the whole culture thing. Are there going to be race riots at the shows?" We were like, "No, man! Just fucking believe in what we're doing here."

When the time came, those were some of the best shows that Anthrax has ever done because the crowds were insane. They were ready for it. Metal fans are smart, and they got it. You have to give metal fans credit. They understood how important that was and how real it was—there was no bullshit there.

The people wanted this to happen, and they loved the fact that it could even exist because we were crossing all these lines that people said couldn't be crossed. I loved that. You could see it in the faces of the audiences every night. There was such a buzz around that tour, and when Public Enemy came out onstage and we played "Bring the Noise" together, it was over. Over.

The days we spent on that tour were some of the most fun I've ever had in my life. We played these intense fucking basketball games right before the show. We'd all eat together and there was a great family vibe. The S1W crew, Public Enemy's on-stage performers, used to do these great things during the show with choreography—and I would learn that choreography with those guys.

I would watch them from the side as they were doing this one cool move, and they'd see me practicing it. I'd say, "How do you do this part? Is it once or twice?" and they'd show me how it was done. It was fucking great, and pretty soon I'd get up on the ramps during their sound check and do it with them.

I watched Public Enemy every night, from beginning to end, because they did such an intense show and I loved it. I knew their routines after a while—all the things that they would do at certain times during the show—and there was a part at the beginning of the show that I really loved. The DJ, Terminator X, would be in his booth above two huge doors, and the music would go, "It's the flavor, it's the flavor, life saver," and the doors would fly open and Flavor Flav would burst out. There was a huge fucking roar every time he did this, and he'd be doing all his moves under a spotlight, and it was an awesome moment, a real highlight of the show.

One night, we were getting ready for the show, and Flavor couldn't make it for some reason. I got this crazy idea that maybe I could take his place for that opening part of the show, when he bursts out of the doors, although obviously I wasn't going to do much rapping, maybe just the first couple of lines.

So, I said to Chuck D at lunch in the food area, "Look, I'm gonna ask you something, and you're probably gonna say no. Let me come out as Flavor tonight." He goes, "What? No!" but I bothered that guy all day until, an hour before the show, he finally said, "All right. Go for it, and we'll see what happens."

So, when showtime came, I covered up as much of my face as possible with the hood of a big, baggy top, snuck onstage, and stood behind the doors beneath the DJ booth. At this point, I realized that maybe it wasn't such a good idea after all. I was shitting in my fucking pants, thinking, "What the fuck am I doing here? Frank, you gotta think more carefully before you do these stupid things."

I was totally out of my element and I had no idea what I was doing. I knew the first couple of lines of the rhyme I was going to do, but I suddenly realized that they might want me to do more than that, in which case I was fucked.

Suddenly I hear the music—"It's the flavor, it's the flavor, life saver"—and the crowd goes nuts on the other side of the doors in front of me. It's my cue, so I smash through the doors and there's a massive roar—and then they go, "Oh," totally disappointed. I think they bought it for like half a second, and then, when I started rhyming, they knew what was up.

I stayed a few seconds and ran offstage, and as I went, I could see Chuck fucking cracking up with laughter. When Flavor heard about it later, he thought it was hilarious. He's a really funny guy, through and through. He'd be backstage in our dressing room, playing drums on Charlie's practice kit all the time. I'd walk in and he'd shout, "Yoooooo! Frankie! What are you doing?" That whole thing was such a great experience.

I became good friends with Chuck D because he's one of the best people on Earth. One time we were at a New York Music Awards event at the Beacon Theater, where Anthrax was getting an award. Public Enemy was there, too, also receiving an award, and there was a great New York vibe. My wife and I said hello to Chuck and we had a great time.

Afterward, we go down to my car in the garage, and it doesn't fucking start. You know how your heart sinks in that situation. I'm kicking it over and kicking it over, and it just won't start, so now I'm frustrated and embarrassed because I'm going to have to get my fucking car towed home. Everybody else is getting in their cars, and I look like the bum here.

You know who comes up to me? Chuck D. He comes up and says, "Hey Frank, what's up?" He sees that my car won't start and says, "Come on, man, I'll drive you home." So we leave the car in the garage and he takes me and my wife home, all the way to our house, which is out of his way. That's the kind of great person he is.

I will remember that a long time. He didn't have to do that. He could have just said, "All right man, good luck with that," but no, he drove us home. He wanted to make sure we got home safe. That's the kind of guy he is. He'll be my brother forever, in a real way.

The bond that Anthrax has with Public Enemy can't be touched. Chuck always says it: it was special. Other people have done similar collaborations, but I'm proud to say that ours was special because it was at a different level. It was deeper, and more serious, and all from the heart.

In May, we played on the Clash of the Titans tour in America. This was the famous tour when Anthrax, Megadeth, and Slayer took turns to headline, with Alice in Chains opening the show—which was funny in hindsight, because they went on to be a huge act in their own right.

Let me tell you something about Alice in Chains. You want to talk about a band that worked hard to get where they got? Nobody knew who they were yet, because they hadn't had a hit, and I remember the audience giving them shit and throwing stuff.

Layne Staley, God rest his soul, was one of the best front men I've ever seen, and took none of that shit from them: he put it right to those fuckers in the crowd. He would go right up to their faces. I loved the way they took on that tour, because they were the underdogs—and they won. They had the grit to stand tall on that tour, and they were the best of people.

Their guitar player, Jerry Cantrell, and I went fishing a lot on that tour. You would never think that, right? I'd watch him play from the side of the stage every night because I thought he was awesome, and we'd get up at fucking six in the morning, renting hotel rooms out and going to lakes to go fishing. I was no good at it, but Jerry taught me all the proper things to do because he was schooled in it. I enjoyed it. It was a fun thing that took us off the tour, and we'd have some laughs and a good time.

I watched every band play on that tour. If we were headlining that night, I'd watch all the bands before we went on and check out the vibe of the crowd. Or if we opened, I watched Megadeth and Slayer afterward. It was just a complete party vibe, and we knew it was a special tour. For me, that was just a bunch of guys who grew up together in this business. It was the celebration. The movement was coming together and we all wanted a stake in it.

Clash of the Titans was the first time we got to hang out with Slayer. We'd played shows with them before, and I would go and see them every time they played in New York, but we'd never spent much time with them apart from a quick hello. The same was true with Megadeth—we didn't really see them much until Clash of the Titans because we'd always been so fucking busy.

Anthrax never really stopped touring in this period of our career. The tour before that was Public Enemy, and I remember being in the dressing room when the idea of the Clash of the Titans tour was brought up.

We'd been on the road nonstop, and I remember thinking, "We have to do this, of course, but when are we going to take a breath here?" because I was so tired. Of course, it made total sense, and we wanted to be a part of it because we wanted to represent our music. It would be great for the band, and great for metal. At the same time, though, we were exhausted. That's the life of a touring musician for you.

The payoff was the lifelong friendships, though. I'm close with Kerry King, and there's no bullshit between us—it's a really honest friendship. In fact, I'm close with all the Slayer guys. Tom Araya is one of life's better people, and I jammed with Dave Lombardo a few years later when we did the Metal Allegiance dates. He's such a soulful, nice guy with so much talent. All of that band have always been close with Anthrax.

We've toured with Slayer so many times since then, and we shared some experiences that you might not expect. For example, every now and then I'd hear Tom playing an acoustic guitar and singing in their dressing room, so I'd go in and pick up another one and we'd jam together. Another time, someone was playing the piano in their room, and Tom and Joey Belladonna were singing together. It sounded beautiful, and I totally get that you would never think that those two together would sound so good. It was a really great blend of voices. The two bands and crews have become really close after so much touring together, and we look out for each other.

As for Kerry, he's dangerous—for my liver! He and Jägermeister are scary fun together. I've literally had to run away and hide out sometimes, but Kerry always sends someone to find me. A guy walks in and says, "Where's Bello? Kerry wants him," and that's that. I go in there and the Jägermeister is cold, and the next thing you know, I'm fucked up.

Those shots sneak up on you like a motherfucker and you're hungover like a bastard the next day. The fog brain is terrible. There've been so many days when I've woken up on a Slayer tour and immediately puked. You think, "Why did I do this again?"

Another curveball came our way when we got to appear on *Married…with Children*, the TV show. If you don't know *MWC*, check it out immediately, because it's fucking hilarious. It's a comedic sitcom about a dysfunctional family, the Bundys, and it was a great experience. They made it so easy for us, and it was a valuable lesson for me in other ways, too.

Missi Callazzo from Megaforce made the call over there, saying that we were big fans, and if we could do anything on the show, to let us know. They came back with a script, and it was easy as that, incredible as that sounds. We all loved the script and they were all into us being on the show.

I was friends with Christina Applegate—who plays the Bundys' daughter, Kelly—before we did the show, because she dated a friend of mine. I remember Christina said, "You're really doing this?" and I said, "Yes, we are!" We'd been on tour for so long that getting to tap into this thing on the side felt like a real celebration.

They flew us out and put us up in a hotel. The whole thing was very Hollywood and cool. I was awestruck because I couldn't believe it was happening, especially on top of *Persistence* going gold and doing all those great tours through 1991. All of a sudden we're at a sound stage, rehearsing at a table read with the whole cast, headed up by Ed O'Neill, who plays Al Bundy, the dad, and who is a very serious, accomplished actor even though the character of Al Bundy is such a clown.

Can you imagine Anthrax at a table read in Hollywood? It was all very surreal. We were saying our lines, and the people around us were fucking laughing as we did it. It was really working, and even when a line didn't work, we would see the writers scribble it out and come up with a new one right on the fly. It was totally intimidating, because you'd think, "That went well," and they said, "It coulda went better. Here's a new line."

So we rehearsed the show and got it up on its feet—sorry for the actor talk. We did the blocking, which is where everybody practices where they're going to stand and moves through all the scenes. After they made sure that every line was right, we did two live recordings on a Friday, in front of an audience. Some of our good friends were there, which added to our anxiety, but we knew the script was great so we were really excited.

The first take went great. We had a couple of hours' break before the second taping, and they changed at least three or four of my lines in the break, because they wanted them to be stronger. I was like, "Really? That line went over good," but they said, "No, no, we have a better one." So I had to learn my lines again in that two-hour break—and they were right, because the crowd went fucking nuts for the new lines.

When it was done, we were so happy. The cast were congratulating us—"You did great," and all that—and then the greatest thing happened. They said to us, "The whole cast and crew is going to the restaurant next door for a party. We want to invite you over."

Now, the reason why this was so important was that I had a secret mission, which I'll confess to now. My goal right off the bat was to hang out with Ed O'Neill, because I knew he'd done theater in New York and I wanted to hear about that. I had recently started to study acting, and I wanted to understand the craft better. What I wanted was some time alone with Ed, just to share a beer and hear his thoughts on the acting profession.

So we get there, and everything that you imagine would be cool in that situation was right there. The food was great, the drinks were great, we're all having great laughs with the cast, and then I see Ed go up to the bar and order a beer. This is my moment, so I make a beeline for him and sit right next to him.

"Ed," I say. "Could I talk to you about theater?"

He's into it, so we go straight into a long talk about his theater days. We share a beer, and that beer turns into another beer, and we're going back and forth. I told him I'm studying with a famous acting coach, Bill Esper, and he tells me he knows Bill, too. Then he's talking about the different actors that he knows in New York and I ask, "Who is the weirdest person to work with?"

He laughs and tells me about this very famous film star that you've definitely heard of. I can't say his name because I'll get killed, but my fucking jaw is hanging right open because the guy he's talking about is such a huge name.

"You know," says Ed, "we were doing this play together, and I can't believe how tight with his money he was. He wanted to be paid for the littlest thing. I had a beer in his apartment—and he wanted me to pay him back for it! It was such a surreal thing…I felt so weird about it. I never expected that from him."

Then he told us that Anthrax did really great in the recording that night, and started asking me about the tours we did. Then he said, "Well, you're obviously successful, because you've come on this show as a little side thing." I said, "Ed, make no mistake, being on this show is huge for us and our career. I know this is a job for you, but for us, this is a highlight of our lives." He laughed and said, "I kinda got that vibe!"

So I got my moment with Ed O'Neill, and it was a wonderful experience. Oh, and who else was hanging out with us that night? Clint Eastwood and Morgan Freeman! Ed introduced us to them, and if you think my mind was blown before, it was truly blown after that.

Our episode of *Married…with Children* went out on February 23, 1992, and I love watching it from time to time. You can see our parts of the show online.

Let me talk to you about acting. I've done quite a bit of studying over the years, although it's never got in the way of my career as a musician—but you know what, the two areas of my life overlap in several ways. An example of that overlap is that, for me, I feel that putting together an acting part is like writing a song. Without wanting to get too actor-ish here, it's about putting the character together with a verse, a chorus, a bridge—and every piece needs to be lived. When you have all that down, you've worked out your character just like you work out a song.

When you do a play, rehearsals with the other actors in the ensemble are just like working on a song with a band in a practice room. You'll work on the character, and expand it, and try different things, and that feeling is just as satisfying as getting a song figured out in a band.

I didn't get into acting for the fame. We all know that fame is bullshit. Someone gets famous, they get the accolades, the pat on the back—fuck all that. I want to get to the meat, to the core, to the substance of what life is. We've had some fame in Anthrax and it was fine, but it didn't mean anything because it's not what I'm looking for. It wasn't about the money, either. If I got paid for acting, then great, but that wasn't my primary objective.

I'm looking for the next high onstage, maybe because I've never really done drugs. The stage is my high, and the way to be convincing onstage is to have the goods. Do your work first and then hit the stage. Write a good song, or make sure you have a good part that is exactly what you want it to be, and then bring it out. Get a character and give them a life, complete with the little things that make up the spice of life.

When you get to perform your creation, that's the ultimate rush. Once you have your great song or part, you get to go onstage and show it to people. You make it live, and that's the payoff. A director liking what you did with a character is exactly the same as the fans liking what you did with a song. It's all about experimenting and trying new things, and there's nothing like it—as long as you prepare, of course, because I truly believe in preparation.

This is all high-stakes stuff that requires courage, which I love. You have to walk a highwire to do this, and you could fall on your fucking face at any second. I love that energy. I don't want to come off the high-wire because I live for it.

Like I said before, I studied with a respected coach, Bill Esper, at his acting studio in New York. I never acted at school, but I've seen a lot of plays in my life, starting when I was seventeen or eighteen, when I used to go down to Broadway, and I think that's why the idea came to me that I could try doing it myself.

I studied the Meisner Technique with Bill. The other way to study is to go to the Actors Studio founded by Lee Strasberg, where you learn the Method. I studied that, too, because I thought it was important to have both sides. I liked studying, because it was all about living in the moment, which I love.

The best way I can describe Meisner is that it's based on living in the moment in circumstances that aren't real. I can bury my head in a character and put the necessary ingredients into him. Where does he live? Where is he coming from? Before you walk through the door, who are you? You can't just walk into a scene with your lines learned. That would never work.

Bill Esper would nail me immediately if I looked like I didn't completely know who my character was. He would say, "Stop!" right after I'd said my first line. "Turn around!" he'd say, in this great big theater voice that I loved but was totally intimidated by.

Imagine this great, talented man who looked like a professor. I loved that he could tear me down but then put me back together again on the other side. I'd be better for that. You gotta be ready for that. I remember some people in that class who didn't take that well, but personally, if I'm paying to learn how to do this—and it wasn't cheap—I'll take it seriously.

Again, I don't want to come off like a pretentious actor, but I think that acting is the ultimate stripping down of your personality. You strip yourself away until you're fucking raw. Stepping on a stage is about learning about yourself because it really digs into the dark, emotional parts of you, and it makes you humble. I guess I was looking at that time to find out who I was, and I really found that out. That knowledge opened doors for me because it meant that I could live in other people.

When I was in class with Bill, he really went deep into who I was. "Living truth" is his whole thing, and I'm a big proponent of that because I want to live my truth day by day, minute by minute. I did a two-year, part-time program with Bill, but I had to leave for the second part of the second year because Anthrax was going on tour. He was totally cool with that, though, and told me that I could always come back and finish.

Bill was very friendly. Again, I come back to the word "nurturing": a definite father figure who taught me a lot, not only about acting but also about myself. For me, acting was all about digging deep into myself, just as this book is. When you read these words, you're seeing me stripped to the bone.

•••

I BOUGHT A CONDO around this time, mainly as a storage facility, like I said before. My brother Anthony was my caretaker while I was away, and he used to take his girlfriends there. He was always good with the ladies. I told him, "Dude, that's fine with me. Do whatever you want to do—just clean it up before I get back." Then I'd come home from a tour, lay down on the bed, and suddenly a fucking used rubber would be stuck to my hand.

I'd call him up and say, "What the fuck is this? I love you, Anthony, but you've gotta clean up in here. I don't care whom you

Me and Charlie, who has always been like a brother to me. Thanks to his example, I became a dedicated musician.

Anthony may have looked tough, and he could be a ball-buster when he wanted to, but at the same time he was a sweet kid and the very best of us.

Teresa and me with my grandmother Bernadette Benante, who I knew as Tina Babes. I'll never forget what she did for me.

*Joe Piacquadio, or "Uncle
Joe" as I know him. What
he taught me about being
a decent man could fill a
entire book. I owe him a
huge debt of gratitude.*

*The famous Joe's Deli in the Bronx, where I worked for years, even in the early days of
Anthrax. Man, the things I saw there would make a pretty hilarious sitcom.
In fact, that's a pretty good idea, now I come to think of it...*

*My mom, Rose, who has
always been there when
I need her.*

This is what happens when you try a new set of strings—they chew up your fingers.

My friend and hero Lemmy, having a smoke backstage somewhere, when Anthrax were supporting Motör-head. I treasure the times I spent with him, just hanging out and talking shop. I was always fascinated by his bass playing—there was something about the way he picked the strings that I always loved, because it was unique to him. He looks pretty serious in this picture, and in fact a lot of people were intimidated by him because of who he was, but once you got to know him, you quickly realized what a cool guy he was.

Look at the excitement on my face. How many bassists can say they got to play live with Lemmy?

My safe home is on the stage, communicating with people.

Andy Buchanan

Saying goodbye to a few close friends at the end of a show.

Andy Buchanan

It's always fun being with Chuck D. There's always something to laugh about —in this case, my Bozo the Clown hair.

Andy Buchanan

Anthrax with Alice Cooper, one of the sweetest guys in the whole of rock music. Look how awestruck I am in this pic.

What's going on with my tongue here? It's pure adrenaline that makes me do this. This is why my back is fucked up and I need a chiropractor. Fortunately, I've learned to wear the right shoes when I do this—they really help, believe it or not. The photographer, my friend Andy Buchanan, calls this move "Air Bello."

Andy Buchanan

This is my primal scream! I'm literally slamming the E note here.

Andy Buchanan

On stage with Rob and John. Note my tattoo of Anthony, which is my way of saying "You're always with me."

Both sides of my personality, in one pic. The happy smile, and the "Fuck you!"

I admire the hell out of Lady Gaga. Calling her a pop artist doesn't do her justice. A real highlight of my career came when I was backstage and she shouted my name, even though we'd never met before.

I have a picture of two dressing-rooms backstage at Seth Meyers' late-night TV show. One says "Anthrax" and the other says "Robert De Niro." Look at our faces. This was a career highlight for us.

I felt different, I looked different and I played bass different when I was in Helmet. You can see me really digging in here, and enjoying the hell out of the show. That's Chris Traynor on stage with me—a great guy and guitar player.

Andy Buchanan

From high-school jazz class to playing in Helmet together, Johnny Tempesta and I still have a good time, wherever we are.

Andy Buchanan

Andy Buchanan

Page Hamilton and me, relaxing after a Helmet show. Being in that band was an important step away from Anthrax for a minute, just to recharge my batteries.

This is the high-register part in the lead section of "I Am the Law," which is a challenge to get right every night. The expression on my face shows you exactly how many issues I have going on in my head, and what kind of crazy person I am. That's what's really going on inside my head, and I'm letting it all out on stage here. I wish everybody had that kind of outlet.

Andy Buchanan

Here we are at Yankee Stadium on the Big Four shows. My grandmother Tina is watching from a private box up on the left, and it was a special show for us because we grew up ten minutes from the stadium. This was huge for us, being right there in the Bronx. We celebrated it all here. We did okay, didn't we?

Andy Buchanan

Andy Buchanan

At one of the Sonisphere shows. Look at the size of the stage—it's actually even bigger than it looks in the picture. When you're on that stage, you know you have to entertain each section of the crowd. I want to connect with everybody, even if they're the length of a football field away.

Andy Buchanan

I'm doing my best impersonation of my heroes Steve Harris and Pete Way here. You can see in my face that I'm thinking, "Fuck yeah! This is happening. Let's do this!"

Andy Buchanan

My comrades in the Big Four. I'm between Lars and James; Scott is right upfront; I can see Charlie and Rob and Joey in there too. Jeff Hanneman, the riff master, is there too—God rest his soul. I loved that guy. He left way too early.

We're at the Dimebash here, organized every year by Dime's girlfriend Rita Haney.
Dave Grohl is an excellent cook—he's smoking meat here. He's a great guy.

I took Brandon to see Cheap Trick, just to show him who my idols were when I was growing up,
and Rick Nielsen was so sweet to both of us.

Andy Buchanan

*I'm at the end of a song
here, holding a note so
it rings out, and saying
to people, "Let's do this
together!" See the reaction
of the kids at the front?
That's what it's all about.*

Andy Buchanan

In Sofia in Bulgaria, where they shot the Big Four DVD. The culmination of all our hard work.

This is backstage at Yankee Stadium, outside the Yankees' dressing rooms. It was huge for me to be on that hallowed ground. Not a lot of people get to see that, so I wanted the moment documented so that Brandon can look back on it in his later life. This was taken after we came off stage, so I felt like I was on cloud eleven.

This picture says, "This is what it's all about."

What can you say about this? A bad hair day, mid-headbang?

Andy Buchanan

Andy Buchanan

Praying to the god of music, whoever he or she is. Music saved my life, and maybe it saved yours too.

Andy Buchanan

We are all one.

fuck, but I just found a used condom with your dried-up load in it! What are you doing?" Of course, we were both laughing our balls off at the same time. It sounds disgusting, but it's such a good memory that I recall with all love and kindness, and it makes me feel close to him when I think of it.

While my real-life brother was enjoying life, me and my band brothers were going through some changes. Anthrax had a new singer, John Bush, a great friend of ours who had been in the band Armored Saint. A new phase of Anthrax's career was about to begin.

None of that really matters, though, in comparison to what was about to happen to me and my family.

10
Anthony

THIS IS GOING TO be a difficult chapter to write, because the biggest tragedy of my life so far hits me right in the middle of it. Bear with me. It helps me to talk to you about it.

You know, we had some good and bad times right after we switched singers from Joey Belladonna to John Bush. We signed to Elektra, which was huge for us, but as has been well documented elsewhere, the album we did for them in 1993—*Sound of White Noise*—didn't do as well commercially as *Persistence of Time*, released three years before. I thought the combination of John's voice and our music made for a fucking heavy record, and a lot of people love that album. I know why, too, because everything was right about it.

With Bush, it was a new band and a new era. I enjoy both incarnations of Anthrax myself, and it all made sense at the time. That's our history, and I'm happy with it because it got us where we are today. We're not afraid to try new things. We had the balls to do a Public Enemy song. We had the balls to record "I'm the Man." We're a wild card, and I'll never back down. I want us to be different: I don't want to be just another run-of-the-mill metal band. There's an edge to us because you never know what the fuck we're going to do. I like the unknown and the mystery.

With all that said, I know a lot of people look at Anthrax as being two different bands because we had two different singers, and I understand that. I understood that some people missed Joey. On top of that, times were changing, musically, and maybe we just didn't fit in.

We had some bad luck with our record companies, too: Elektra didn't really promote the next album, *Stomp 442*, in 1995. It didn't do too well, and we faced a pretty tough back end of the nineties for that reason.

But like I said, we still had some good times. We still had our sense of humor, and we still had a solid brotherhood with our fellow bands. I have a particular story that I want to share with you now—a bright light of fun in a period of my life that got very dark very quickly.

We were playing in San Francisco one night, and what do you know, our buddies James, Lars, and Kirk came to the show. This was the night I mentioned a while back when James said "I couldn't hear the bass" just digging in and busting my balls. It was a party night, and Charlie, Scott, and I went barhopping with those guys. It turned into one of the greatest nights of my life because it was so much fun, with the ultimate example of ballbusting in the aftermath.

So we were out on the town with Metallica, and different people were driving us 'round, and at one point we were in a vehicle that Lars owned. He had a designated driver taking care of us, and we were in the back, feeling pretty buzzed. We'd go into every bar we came across and get more loaded, then get back in the car. I have no idea how many stops we made, but every time we were laughing our asses off.

After a while, of course, I started throwing up because I'm such a pathetic lightweight with booze. The first time I puked, I held all the goop in my hands and then threw it out the window. After that,

I puked out of the window—and after a while, the whole side of Lars's car was covered in my vomit. Sorry, Lars. It was horrible, but everyone else was laughing their balls off, of course.

Fortunately, I have the ability to throw up and then start drinking again, so every time it happened, I'd go into the next bar, head to the bathroom, wash my mouth out and then carry right on doing shots. It's like a superhuman ability that I have, which served me well when I got to know Dimebag Darrell, as you'll see.

After a few hours of this, we were in the truck, driving who knows where, and someone said, "We should jam!" We were all fucking out of our minds with booze, and of course it seemed like a great idea, so we all said, "Yeah! Let's fucking turn it up, it'll be so metal!"

The next obvious question was "Where are we going to jam in San Francisco at this time of night?" because it was the early hours by now and everywhere was closed. Someone said, "Let's go to Kirk's house!" because we knew he had a rehearsal space there. Kirk had left earlier, but that didn't deter us, because we were fucked up and not thinking straight.

So about six or seven of us—me, Scott, James, Charlie, Lars, and a few others—rolled up to Kirk's house in two cars. We were trying to be quiet so we wouldn't wake anyone up. He had a studio in the basement, and the door was open, so we went in there and turned on the lights.

Holy shit. Kirk had a full band setup in there: Marshall amps, drums, mics, guitars, everything. We were like "Yes!" and within two minutes everybody had a guitar strapped on and every Marshall was turned up to ten. Can you imagine the volume in there? It was the loudest fucking thing you could possibly think of. I don't know what the fuck we were playing, we were just screaming shit and raging. Just imagine Metallica and Anthrax drunk out of our minds, laughing our asses off and making a huge, huge noise.

Suddenly I look through the window of the basement and I see Kirk's face. He's bending down, looking in to see what's happening, and I hear him shout, "What the fuck!" He's pointing at us and I think, "Oh, shit. Kirk's pissed at us. This is his house we're in," and I start feeling really guilty. In his position, I'd be really angry, too.

He asks us to leave, so we all troop out with our heads hanging, like kids at school who did something wrong. Under our breath we're still laughing our asses off, but I was feeling really bad about it, so on the way down the hill from his house I say to Lars, "That sucks, I feel really bad about this."

Lars says, "Maybe we should go back and apologize."

So he and I walk back up the hill to Kirk's front door. Everybody else has gone back to the cars, so it was just us two.

I knock on the door. Nobody's answering.

I ring the bell. Still no answer, so I push it with my foot. I didn't kick it, because I'm not that much of an idiot, I just tapped it. As I'm doing this, I lose my balance and I fall against the door really heavily. It was a beautiful glass door—and I hear this huge crack.

Fuck! The whole thing breaks. I look at the door and there's a massive crack running down it.

Lars and I look at each other with stupid, shocked expressions on our faces—and we take off back to the cars. As we're running, we hear Kirk shouting, "What the fuck, man! What the fuck! You broke my fucking door!"

I woke up the next morning and I had no idea what had happened the previous night. My memory was totally empty. My tour manager came up to me with this worried look on his face.

"Frank, where were you last night?"

I say, "Uh, I think we went out with the Metallica guys and hung out at a bunch of bars. Why?"

He looks at me in this weird way and says, "Dude, is everything okay with you guys?"

I said, "Yeah, why?"

He hands me a fax and says, "This just arrived for you."

I look at this fax—and it's a bill for $13,000 for repairs to Kirk's door.

Suddenly everything came back to me, and I thought, "Holy shit. I can't afford this. There's no way." I was scared shitless, so I called Kirk to apologize and said, "I'm so sorry."

Kirk was cool about it, fortunately. I was prepared to pay the $13,000, in instalments if I had to, but he said, "It's all right, dude. Don't worry about it. Just don't let it happen again!"

You know what? The bill for $13,000 was a prank. It was a scam that someone—I don't know who—had dreamed up, just to fuck with me. There was genuine damage to the door, which had apparently been imported from overseas, but $13,000 was an invented number.

Years later Kirk told people in a web chat that the door cost $850 to repair. That's still a chunk of money, so he was a gentleman for not billing me for it. Some motherfucker really got me good, convincing me that I owed Kirk $13,000. It was the ultimate Pirate Attack.

•••

LET ME TALK TO you now about my brother Anthony.

He was the last of the five Bello kids, and he was born in 1972, so he was eight years younger than me. He was the biggest Anthrax fan and was at every New York show we did. All the guys in the group loved him because he was a good kid.

What's more, he was the best family member of us, the most level-headed, and the peacemaker. When me and my other brother, Chuck, would argue, he would never stand for it. He was a burly kid, and he had a great knockout punch; he could kick either of our asses if he wanted to. You would never fuck with him.

Anthony was almost like my protector, in some ways. He would come to our shows to take care of me. He'd say, "You all right, Frank?" and I'd say, "I'm fine. What are you doing?" and laugh, but I knew it was always done out of love. He was the kind of guy that you'd love to hang out with because he'd always make you feel comfortable. After you talked to him, he'd have your back.

He was very much from the Bronx, with that fight mentality, but he was the nicest guy in the world—until you got to his other side, which you really didn't want to see. He was a fun-loving, good man, but he got involved with some kids from the old Bronx neighborhood that I wish he wouldn't have, and I think that was part of what ultimately happened to him.

I have a great memory of Anthony wearing a tux at a family wedding, dancing to one of those cool old funk songs. He was making a funny scene, just to make everyone laugh. I keep that memory in my head, because it makes me feel good whenever I think of it—but at the same time, it breaks my heart.

On March 25, 1996, our new guitar player Paul Crook was staying at my house because we were working on some music. He was the angel in the house that night. He was sleeping in one of the beds, and I was watching TV in the living room. There was a staircase outside my house, and I could hear when people were walking up to my front door.

Over the volume of the television, I heard someone slam a car door outside and then frantically run up the stairs and bang on my door.

"Frank! Frank!"

I thought, "Who the fuck is that?"

Paul heard it too and came out. I opened the door and it was Charlie.

"You've gotta come," he said. "Anthony's been shot. He's dead."

I fell on the floor. Paul and Charlie picked me up.

"He can't be dead," I said. "He can't be. There's no way. He's alive."

Charlie told me what had happened. Anthony had been shot, and he hadn't survived. He drove me to the murder scene. I was sitting in his car, screaming and crying at the top of my lungs. He was crying, too.

We get to the scene, and it's like one of those television shows, with a crowd and an ambulance and cops everywhere, in this area that I knew called Morris Park Avenue in the Bronx, where we all grew up. I see my mother, looking lost. I remember I went up to her, and in my visual of her now, looking back, she seemed to be glowing, the sense of loss was so profound.

I embraced her and I didn't know what to say, because there were no words. The sorrow was said through our hearts. We couldn't understand how this happened. That was the hardest thing to deal with, right there, just holding her.

I looked over at the crime scene and I saw Anthony's body, covered with a sheet. The sheet wasn't long enough to cover his sneakers that I knew so well, and his blood was on them. To this day, that image is in my head.

We asked all the questions that anyone would ask in that situation. The murderers had taken off from the scene and dumped the gun right around the block. The police had all the information they needed, fortunately, because they had found an eyewitness.

Everyone else who was there at the time, cowards that they are, and I hope they read this book, denied seeing anything.

Those people should be ashamed of themselves. We all have families. How could they see that happen, and let it go, even all these years later? We had connections in that area, and we knew that there were a lot of witnesses to what happened, but only one person was brave enough to testify.

I went all through the stages that people go through after this kind of terrible event. First pain, then anger, and so on. You deal with those, and after that, you want justice. In fact, all you want is justice. I didn't want my brother's life to be in vain. I wanted the person, or persons, who took my brother's life to be held accountable. That's all you want, as the family of the victim, because you need closure.

We met with the DA, we met with the detective, we had everything we needed. In the court case that followed, the eyewitness came forward in the preliminary trials. Everything was moving toward a conviction. The court scenes were exactly like a Martin Scorsese movie, where you had the wannabe gangsters on one side of the courtroom and my family and friends on the other.

When we walked into these proceedings, it was very intimidating because these were tough guys, but we were in so much pain, and needing justice to be served so badly, that we knew we had nothing to lose. Absolutely nothing. What was the worst they could do to me?

I felt like I wasn't Frankie from Anthrax anymore. I didn't give a fuck about anything. I didn't care about anything other than getting closure by getting these scumbags that did it behind bars. I had total tunnel vision about it. Closure for my family was more important than closure for me, because they were in so much pain, crying day and night.

I remember the first day of preliminary trial. The intimidation factor was there from all the wannabes. As they looked over at us, there were a lot of smirks and dismissive gestures from them, almost like they were saying, "How dare you be here?" to us.

But if there's one thing you need to know about the Bello family, it's that we're fucking fighters, and unafraid of anybody. Anthony was the most fearless of us all; he would take on the biggest men. If he was in the right, he was in the right, and he would win. The coward who killed Anthony had to take a gun because he couldn't beat him up. I'll say that straight out. There was no reason to take a life like that.

So the courtroom cops are watching us now; they're on high alert. They know it's a dangerous situation. The proceedings continue, the lawyers talk, they announce that the eyewitness is going to be brought in for the next session.

The next time in court is even more tense, because we know the eyewitness is going to be there. All the bad guys are there; the murderer's friends are all there. The eyewitness comes in, with guards protecting him, and identifies Anthony's killer, who is right there in the courtroom in front of us.

I'm sitting there with my mother, my aunt Laurie, my brother Chuck, my sisters, and some of our friends, standing in for our brother Anthony, looking for justice and closure. Now, as the murderer is standing there in cuffs, he looks over at us—and like he's in the movies, the motherfucker snickers at us.

Instantly I'm on my feet, and so is Chuck. We're about to go for it, because at this point I could not give a fuck. What is jail gonna do to me? If someone kills me, do you think I care? I was prepared to do anything I could at this point.

But our mother and Laurie grab us, calm us down, and make us sit back down, which was the right thing to do because the tough guys were looking at us, and this thing was going to happen.

Cooler heads prevailed, fortunately, because the judge would have been pissed at us, and we didn't want that.

The judge asked the eyewitness to explain what had happened. The guy said, "I saw the accused take the gun and shoot three times into Anthony Bello. After the first shot, the victim said, 'Don't shoot again. You've proved your point,' but the gunman shot him twice more." Hearing the scene being described, all I could think was, "Why can't I be invisible right now so I can go over there and destroy this person?"

By the way, this story is not intended to make me sound like a tough guy—please don't interpret it that way. It's about being there for your brother. The guy who killed him felt no sorrow, he felt no remorse, and he was standing right in front of me, laughing at us.

After a couple more of these court proceedings, we got a call from the detective. They couldn't find the witness. He'd disappeared. It turned out that he'd moved to Florida because he'd been intimidated. In other words, they got to him.

The case was dismissed. I know it sounds like something out of the movies, but it was real, and it happened to us.

I lost my shit after that.

I'm going to be really honest with you here. My family doesn't know this. My wife doesn't know this. I went out to buy guns and then, late at night, I went out searching for the guy who killed Anthony. I drove around the specific areas where I knew he would be. I knew what he looked like, but I didn't find him, and later I found out that he had also moved away.

I wasn't the Frank Bello that you guys know. I was out of my fucking mind, and I didn't know me anymore. In my bones, I know that if I'd have located this guy, I would have taken care of it. Again, I'm not saying that to sound like a tough guy or a crazy person.

There was no justice any other way. I have no faith in the criminal justice system. Of course, I know there are good people out there working hard in that system, but it's not what people think it is.

A couple of weeks later, something pulled me out of it. Call it divine intervention, call it the spirit of Anthony, but I began to think rationally and stopped searching for the guy. I knew that if I did what I wanted to do, there would be serious repercussions—and although I literally didn't give a shit if I died at that point, I couldn't put my mom and my grandmother and the rest of my family through that.

Another consideration was that I was now in a serious relationship with Teresa, who is now my wife. She's the best girl in the world, and I knew that I'd lose her if I went through with it. Most importantly, I realized that if Anthony could see what I was doing, he would slap me 'round the head and say, "What the fuck are you thinking? Go home. You want to put our mom through all this again, right after what happened to me?"

Now that I'm age fifty-six, not thirty-one, and I'm a dad and a husband, I thank God that divine intervention—or whatever you want to call it—made me see a little light in all that chaos. I'm very happy that I didn't choose that way. I don't think I'd be here talking to you now, if I'm honest.

I've never told anybody this before now because I was scared of who I was. I didn't know I had that darkness in me, and I never want to revisit it—never again. Therapy has helped me to understand why I did it, and why not to do it again.

Once you have a loss like that, it will never leave you. You can compartmentalize it, and place it over on one side, but it's still always with you. If I watch a violent movie, I have to calm myself down, because I've seen the real thing. Right after it happened, I couldn't watch anything of that nature.

I still feel a lot of guilt about Anthony. He had a lot of friends, and if I'd been murdered like that, it would have been a different story. He would have taken care of the guy who did it, without a doubt, because that's the kind of guy he was. I also feel guilty that I wasn't there for him when he needed me as a kid, because I was always away on tour. I wish I would have spent more time with him, and it pains me to this day.

I want it to be understood that my brothers in Anthrax supported me one thousand percent through this. They all came to the wake. Anthony was Charlie's nephew, of course, but the other guys stepped up to support me, too.

We played in Japan a couple of weeks later. The full band was required, and the dates couldn't be postponed. If we hadn't done that tour the band would have lost a huge amount of money, so I agreed to go as long as the guys knew that I needed to be left alone when I wasn't playing the shows. That's what I did—I stayed in my hotel room, crying my eyes out. Emotionally, I wasn't there; I wasn't even me. Mike Monterulo flew to Japan with me, knowing that I wasn't in my right mind: I'll forever be grateful to him for that.

At one point I ran into Scott, and he gave me a huge hug and said, "Thank you for doing this. I just want you to know, from all of us in the band, that you didn't have to do this tour, and we're so grateful that you did." They were there for me, and the fans were there for me, too. They all helped me get through that horrible time.

At times over the intervening twenty-five years, I've considered searching for Anthony's murderer, but I'm a family man now, and I also believe in karma. Every dog has his day, and I can't go back to that place because I'm responsible for my son. That's my mission, right there, and it's my only mission—to raise him the right way.

I wrote a song called "Pieces" in Anthony's honor, which was a hidden track on our album *Volume 8*, which came out in 1998.

Paul Crook really helped me with producing it, and Charlie played guitar. A lot of people react to this song because they've had losses themselves, and they feel the pain of the song. I appreciate that, and if it helps them through their pain, I'm happy, because that's what music is about.

The lyrics are below, and they sum up what I feel about Anthony, and how he's still with me. I was talking to him as I wrote them because I never got the chance to say goodbye to him. It's a song of hope, and it really helped me, and it helped other people too. I've had so many people come up to me and tell me that it helped them through the death of a father or an uncle or a brother.

It's my primal scream, and I have a hard time listening to it because it takes me back to that day when I wrote it, with my tears falling on the lyrics as I wrote them.

The sun is shining off his face again
Another day to reflect
I hope you understand
Looking for the sign that lets me know
That you're fine
That you're fine
You just found your way back home

Feel you with me, feel you everywhere
Yelling up at the sky
Won't get me anywhere
So take me someplace
Where I will always know
That you're fine
That you're fine
You just found your way back home

Who's to tell me I have to let it go?
I need to say this, have to let you know
I'll be here waiting for our souls to meet
I'll be here waiting for your call to me

Anthony, I know you're home
Right beside me, all alone
Anthony, I have so much to say
In my heart, you will always remain
I'll never be alone

Maybe I'm blind and
Maybe I don't wanna see
Reality staked its final claim in me
Lessens the sting when
I think I know
That you're fine
That you're fine
You just found your way back home

I question my faith
I question everything
I need to know if this is all there is
So take me someplace
Where I will always know
That you're fine
That you're fine
You just found your way back home

Who's to tell me I have to let it go?
I need to say this, I have to let you know
I'll be here waiting for our souls to meet
I'll be here waiting for your call to me

Anthony, I know you're home
Right beside me, all alone
Anthony, I have so much to say
In my heart, you will always remain
Anthony, my brother, my friend
I'll be with you once again
Anthony, my heart holds your flame
It will always light your name

I'll never be alone
I'll never be alone
I'll never be alone
I'll never be alone.

For Anthony Bello, 1972–1996

11
Cathartic Days

I N MY LIFE I'VE been through a lot of pain—emotional, with the loss of Anthony and other loved ones, and physical, whether that means getting my ass kicked as a kid or just by life itself. I've been through poverty. I've been through death.

None of that has stopped me permanently. All those things are temporary, and although they hurt, I get back up. You've probably experienced some of those things yourself, and if you have the right spirit, you'll win through. There's always a way to get out of a hole—you just have to find it.

Learn how to pivot. Move on. When ill fortune comes your way, a better path will open up somewhere—you just have to keep looking for it, even though it's scary.

For me, I had my band of brothers in Anthrax to support me, and I had Teresa, who was my rock all the way through the trauma of losing Anthony. A year or so after his passing, I could think relatively straight again, and I was actually enjoying life. I kissed her goodbye one more time and we headed out on tour for the most chaotic time of our lives—with Pantera.

If you like a drink, why not pour yourself a cold one while I tell this story? You're going to love it, even though it takes place after the worst episode of my entire life. In some ways, what follows was a part of the healing that I needed.

Touring has never been too exhausting for me because I don't drink much, so I'm not hungover. The only time I've come home from a tour and spent time recovering was after this tour with Pantera, when we rolled through America in late 1997. After that, I needed to get my health back, for reasons that you'll understand.

What you have to understand is that Pantera were the Van Halen of metal. The death of Eddie Van Halen came in October 2020, as I was writing this book, and it wasn't just the passing of another rock star—he was bigger than that. He was the innovator of a whole way of life, and a musician who took rock music to the top of a whole new mountain. I don't think anyone has ever done that in the way that Eddie did it. He added a sweetness and a creativity to guitar playing that made it stand out from every other guitarist.

So, when I describe Pantera as the Van Halen of metal, I mean it very specifically. Dimebag Darrell and his brother Vinnie Paul lived life to the fullest, like Eddie did, and they were fun-loving people, like Eddie was. To say they partied hard is the mother of all understatements, but at the same time they were real people—no one was more real than Pantera.

Anthrax wasn't a sober group, but we weren't big drinkers when we came into this tour. As soon as we got into the Pantera vibe, that changed. I'll say right off the bat that it was impossible to keep up with their alcohol consumption, but we tried, believe me.

It started slow. Before our set, we'd go into Pantera's dressing room. Dimebag would say "Let's go!" and pour some shots of his cocktail, the Black Tooth Grin, which was a shot of Crown Royal whiskey flavored with a dash of Coke. I'd never had one of these before I met Dimebag, so I had one or two, and then I thought

I was done. That was my first mistake, because with Pantera, you were never done, ever, even though you had a show to do.

I got into the habit of having quite a few drinks with them before I went onstage, and I was worried about that, so I'd be throwing down water and coffee before we went on to try and sober up a little. After a few shows, I thought, "I can't drink this much before the set anymore."

I was usually very conscious of not drinking before we went onstage, because I want to give the audience my very best performance. I feel I'm cheating them if I can't play my best, or if I fuck up because I'm drunk—so before we went onstage, I'd drink only two or three shots with Pantera and then find an excuse to leave, just to get away.

By the second leg of this tour, there was even more reason not to drink because I was on antibiotics for a weak stomach. The doctor told me, "Absolutely no liquor, or you'll undo all the work we've put in to make your stomach better." To do that, I literally had to hide from Dimebag and the rest of Pantera, because every time I saw them, they would pour booze down my throat.

I'd be hiding at the back of Anthrax's tour bus, and Dimebag would come and find me with a bottle of Crown and say, "Let's go!" It was all meant with a kind heart, and I could never say no to Dimebag. I'd be throwing up in front of him, and when I was done, he'd say, "You good? Let's go!"

Even if I did manage to avoid drinking before we went onstage, at some shows, Dimebag would walk out onto our stage with a huge tray of Black Tooth Grins for us to drink. We'd be in mid-song, and suddenly the crowd would go crazy and the spotlights would all move to the side of the stage. We'd think, "What the fuck?" and look over, and he'd be standing there, holding the tray and laughing his ass off. Guess what we had to do? Finish the whole tray.

I knew all this booze was bad for me, but at the same time it was pure rock and roll. Anthrax never really lived that Van Halen-style party life until this tour, and it was so much fun that we welcomed it. It was the right time, it was with the right people, and you couldn't have a better ambassador for that life than Dimebag Darrell. We were truly close with those guys; they were our brothers.

After the shows, Pantera always had bags and bags of Taco Bell. Every single night, I'm not kidding. If you have a bad gut like I had at the time, it's just going to explode. I was living on Imodium and Pepto-Bismol. That was our way of life for that tour. There were no nights off. There was no night when you couldn't drink—that's the truth.

One day toward the end of the first leg of the tour, I looked at myself in the mirror in the hotel and thought, "I look fucking gray." My skin had this weird gray sheen, and I was quite concerned...but I kept on drinking.

The other thing that these guys did was gamble, and I don't mean a little bit of gambling to fuck around, but hardcore gambling with huge sums of money. We played blackjack and craps, mostly. I'd watch Pantera play from the side of their stage and as I was sitting there, someone from their crew would bring over some shots. After they came offstage, it was "let's go!" again: time to rage back in their dressing room.

Then someone would shout "casino!" and we'd head to Pantera's bus, where they'd mapped out a full-on casino. We'd pile in there and start gambling, drinking, and, you guessed it, eating Taco Bell. This posse of drunken maniacs would roll through the night, living it up.

We'd go to real casinos along the way, taking up blackjack tables to ourselves. These guys would be betting one hundred dollars at a time; I tried to keep up at first, but then I backed down and kept my bets down to twenty-five dollars or thereabouts. The bar would be open, and the waitresses kept bringing the drinks, and on we'd rage, all fucking night, every night.

I remember one night when Dimebag was losing a lot of money. His pile of chips was dwindling fast, and when the dealer came up with yet another blackjack, he said, "Now you done took all my money." He was getting a little loud, and he wanted another drink, but it was late and the bar was closed. So, he says, "Now you done took all my money, and now I can't get a drink!" It was one of the great speeches.

Like I said, every night was a party. There was no downtime on that tour. Usually it's not possible to make every single night a party on tour, but Pantera managed it. I've never seen anything like it. It was incredible and I was in awe. They could make things happen, like the time when they got sick of Taco Bell and got McDonald's delivered right into the casino. How do you even do that? Casinos don't let you order food for delivery, and they certainly don't let you eat at the blackjack table. I don't know how they did it, but there I was, biting into a fucking Big Mac right there at the table. Maybe they were spending so much money that the manager turned a blind eye.

After the casino, we'd go back to the Pantera bus, which had a full working bar, and keep going. We'd be blasting out music that we loved and screaming at the tops of our lungs. This was rock and roll.

You see why I call them the heavy metal Van Halen?

After a while a numbness set in. I was starting to get used to this life. It didn't matter if another shot was coming. When it arrived, it was going down. If I had to throw up, I'd run to the bathroom and throw up. I'd wash up and get right back into it. Another shot would be waiting for me and I would do it. "Booze is the healer.

Let's go!" said Dimebag, as I threw another one back because I felt so shitty from the night before.

I often woke up on the Pantera bus in the morning, not in a bunk, but lying on the floor between the rows of bunks. Believe it or not, I'd be clutching a beer when I woke up, so the obvious thing to do was to drink it because I felt so terrible.

When I went home from that tour, my skin was gray and my stomach was fucked—so what was the first thing I did? Buy some whiskey and beers and have a drink, on my own at home. I was so used to it, it seemed like the normal thing to do. Fortunately, I quickly realized that this was a bad idea and stopped drinking for a while so that I could recover. I wasn't becoming an alcoholic, but I definitely needed to dial it down, and that's what I did.

I tell this story with all love, because it was one of the best times of my life. There will never be any band as true as Pantera again. Dimebag and Vinnie are both in my heart and soul. I can't believe they're both gone.

Back in the real world, we had recorded our new album, *Volume 8: The Threat Is Real*, with high hopes after moving on from Elektra and the under-promoted *Stomp 442* record. Our new label was Ignition Records, and although we were really pleased with *Volume 8*, it was doomed because the label lost their funding and went under.

Talk about a string of bad luck. Everyone thinks that Anthrax has had this smooth ride through our career, but I have to stop those people and tell them, no fucking way. These were the dark times. We'd got signed to a deal that we'd been working our fucking asses off to get, and we'd been on the road nonstop, and all of a sudden it comes to a screeching halt, with no money.

Nobody understood it. It was like a slap in the face.

"What? There's no money?"

"Whaddaya mean, there's no money?"

We'd never heard that before because we'd always made a living off of our band. Business was now getting in the way of our art. That was exactly what was happening because we couldn't afford our art. There was just no money anywhere.

You bust your ass to write and put out a record, and you set up the cover art, and you expect the whole cycle to take place, and then they tell you, "There's no money to promote this thing." How were we supposed to tour? People couldn't even get that record because they literally weren't making the physical product. This business is a fucking dick sometimes.

But there's always good news, and the good news for me was that Teresa and I got married on July 18, 1998. I loved Teresa from the moment I met her, but it took me eight years to marry her. I was always on the road, I guess, but that was just an excuse.

The real reason for waiting so long was because I knew I had to make the right choice, as I'd always promised myself that I would never get divorced. I would never do what my mom and dad did. That's why it took me forever to get married, because of the insecurities that I felt after what I saw when I was a kid. I had to make sure that this girl was my best friend and that this was forever. I knew that once I got married, I was married.

Not long after Anthony passed away, the time came, and in the end, it was easy because I knew I'd found the right girl. I did the whole thing right and asked her father first. He loved it, so it was all good.

So, I brought Teresa to a restaurant near her house. Right there in that crowded restaurant, I went on one knee. It was a total surprise to her. She said, "Are you okay?" because she thought I was sick, which makes me laugh now that I think of it, but then I took out the box and she was like, "Oh, my God!" and started tearing up.

It looked like a scene out of a romantic comedy, with everybody applauding. It was one of life's great moments.

We've been a great match. Happiness had been a long time coming at that point in my life, so soon after losing my brother, and my family needed this bit of happy news. I would have proposed to Teresa anyway, but I definitely needed an extra dose of stability and security after what had happened to us. I needed that solid foundation at home so that my mind could open up creatively to making music. That holds true to this day. Teresa is my rock, and without her it's all over for me.

We got married at the Marina Del Ray catering hall, which is right down the road from where Charlie and I grew up. It was the same catering hall that I worked as a waiter on the weekends, in addition to my uncle's deli, when I was a teenager. It's a beautiful spot and a lot of my family members have gotten married there.

We went on a cruise for ten days as our honeymoon, which was great, and then, of course, I was straight back on tour. Teresa really has a lot of patience when it comes to me being away, thank God. Being the partner of a musician that is constantly out on the road requires a lot of strength. You need to be patient, and you need to have a lot of trust.

Because I went on tour so often, it meant that we got to know each other in increments. People say that might have extended our marriage, and maybe that's true. Fortunately, Teresa is the most patient person in the world. She tolerates me, and right off the bat I give her all the credit for that. I'm a high-energy individual, and there's a yin and yang to every marriage. That's something you look for in a life partner—something that completes you—and the truth is that Teresa completes me. She's the complete deal, and everything that I've ever wanted in a woman. She was the girl that I was always looking for.

My wife is mellow, she's thoughtful, she takes her time with things, and she thinks things out, which I don't do enough of. She makes me think, and she's taught me a lot about life over the years. Through her, I know how to deal with a lot of things that I never learned how to deal with in my childhood. She helps me to cope with a lot of things—family stuff, day-to-day stuff, things that can be challenging. She makes me want to be a better man.

Mellow though Teresa is, she'll call it like it is if I need it. She's the most docile person, but she'll absolutely pull the reins in when I need it—and I love that about her. I need that structure in my life because I never really had that as a kid. I think it's really important. She'll say, "What are you doing, Frank? What was that all about?" and that will make me think about things differently. She'll show me a different way to think about things, which is great because I need that. The bottom line is that she makes me see that there's a different side to life.

So, what do I bring to the marriage? Well, I guess I'm a fun guy. I want to make people feel good, and I think I have a nice way of doing that. I'm not perfect by any means, but I do want to make people happy, and she knows that I come from a good place when I do that. I bust balls a lot and I complain about day-to-day things, but I tell fun stories and make sure people enjoy themselves, too. I just want to have fun because life is short, right?

Just as I want to be a good father to my son because of the experiences of my childhood, I also want to be a good husband to Teresa for the same reason. I want to be everything that is the opposite of what I saw back then, and I want that forever.

We lived in my condo until we moved into our current house in 2013. I have to say, I miss condo life, because you get things done for you—there's a maintenance guy who does everything. I know nothing about fixing things, so I was thrown into the fire. I've broken a lot of things while trying to fix them, which sucks.

They should teach you these skills at school. Get rid of algebra and bring in some home maintenance. That would actually be useful. I'm never going to use algebra. I was helping Brandon with it recently, and I didn't have a clue. Be a plumber or an electrician, kids, because that's where the money is.

Like I said before, the back end of the nineties was tough for Anthrax. I'd say 1999 was our least busy year ever. Scott and Charlie reformed S.O.D. and toured, so everything was up in the air with Anthrax. Nobody knew what the fucking deal was. I spent a lot of time playing music by myself because nobody was making any decisions. Where's the record deal? Where's the distribution? Is there a market for us to play if we had a record? All that stuff, and at the time things were different for older metal bands like us, because nu-metal bands like Korn and Limp Bizkit were popular.

So in 1999, and for a chunk of 2000, I just hung out a lot. I jammed with different people and had fun with that. Paul Crook was one of them. We put together a cover band for a little while and played a couple of gigs in Jersey. Paul is a special person to me, because he was in the condo with me the night my brother was murdered. If you believe in fate, and I do, then I think there was a reason he was there that night, because his positive nature was a real comfort to me. He's always been a guy who says, "You can," and he works so fucking hard. People should know that about him.

You know what? I enjoyed being home for a change. I didn't worry much about my finances because I'm very frugal, but they definitely crossed my mind, as they should when you're a responsible person. Thankfully I had made some good investments, but I'm an earner and it's in my nature to work hard. I'm a blue-collar guy and I knew that if the music stopped, I would go and work somewhere and I would succeed. I'd do two jobs. I'd do three jobs. I'd do whatever the fuck it took, and that's the same today. I can't just sit here and wither up and die; it's not gonna happen.

Anyway, this was just a pause for Anthrax. I always knew it was going to come back. It was just a waiting period, and it didn't really feel that long of a wait. Nu-metal didn't worry me because I knew Anthrax could and would pivot if we had to. I'm proud to say that this band can adapt if it needs to, even though we'll always play heavy music.

I always think about what the band needs to do to get through the latest obstacle. I choose to remember the good times, because what's the point of negativity? And I use the word "choose" with good reason, because it is a choice: you can choose to linger in the negative events that have happened, or acknowledge that they happened and move on. I'll fight to get to the next stage of whatever's better. My band are fighters, and we get to where we want to be.

By the end of 2000, we had a new deal with Nuclear Blast and we had a new guitarist on the way, Rob Caggiano. I love that guy; he's a brother from another mother. He's a talented motherfucker with a great ear, whether as a guitar player or as a producer. New songs were getting written into 2001 and we toured with Judas Priest, which was obviously a phenomenal experience for us. They had Tim "Ripper" Owens on vocals at the time, who is another good friend of ours.

On September 11 that year, we were on the tour bus in Nebraska. I usually get up around ten or eleven o'clock when I'm on tour, but I remember being awoken early that morning by shouting from the front lounge, where the TV was. People were yelling, "What the fuck! Oh, my God!" so I jumped out of my bunk and ran in there to see what was going on.

The TV was showing the Twin Towers in New York, right after the first plane had hit. Nobody could understand what was happening: it only became clear when the second one hit. I thought the first one was an accident—in fact, I was praying that it was an accident. None of us thought it could have been done on purpose.

I thought I was watching a horror movie. It was so surreal. I thought I was dreaming. My city, where I grew up, was being torn apart. How could America let these people do this? How could these people get into our airspace? I couldn't believe that this could happen in our country. You saw terrorism everywhere else, but not in America, because we always thought we were safe. We had incidents, sure, but not on this grand scale.

It finally sank in when the TV announcers came on and said that they thought it was a deliberate attack. I was distraught, and also completely drained of energy; it was like the battery went dead inside me. But I was angry as a motherfucker, and I wanted to get home. I read the news reports that said that people were actually jumping out of the windows. The horror of that has never left me.

So, we realized that we were off tour, but at the same time, we were on a tour bus in the middle of fucking Nebraska. What was our status? We didn't know. There was no rhyme or reason to it. There were no flights going home, of course, so we had to drive all the way to New York.

Picture this. Two days later, as we crossed the George Washington Bridge, which has a view of the city skyline, we looked out of the window and saw the huge cloud of smoke over Manhattan. We couldn't understand it. It didn't feel real. Our disbelief and denial was complete. I felt very vulnerable, and helpless; and when I feel helpless, I feel angry.

What did this mean? I didn't know. How did people let this happen? Whose watch was this? Someone let their guard down, and they fucked up somewhere. It was so traumatic, with so much loss of life and families torn apart and the deaths of so many first responders.

All I really remember is that cloud of ash and smoke. It was so horrible. I went down there a year or two later, when they allowed people to go there. I went to a church down there and said a prayer and paid my respects, but I could still smell it. You could literally smell the horror and the pain—a kind of burning sense memory that I can still feel. I pray to God that shit never happens again.

I still feel vulnerable today. The safety blanket that we had is gone forever, and our innocence with it. God rest the souls of everyone we lost, and the first responders who are still dealing with the cancers and other diseases that came from that day twenty years ago. They saved our asses.

Two months later, our good friend Eddie Trunk put together a benefit concert called New York Steel. Twisted Sister and a lot of other great bands were playing as well as us. It was a big deal for Anthrax, because Scott said in jest that we were going to change our name in response to the envelopes of anthrax powder that were being sent through the post. It was almost as if these crazy people were taking our name from us, after we'd built it up into a good thing over so many years. People were asking us if we were going to change it, and because of the resilience of this band, we were like, "Fuck no."

When we walked into the club, which was full of firemen, police officers, and EMTs, I can't tell you how many people came up to us and said, "Don't change your fucking name! Don't let them win! We don't change for nobody!" That was right before our show, so I had this fire in me that gave me fierce fucking energy.

Onstage, we wore these white jumpsuits that said, "We're not changing our name." That's the spirit of Anthrax, right there. When we came out onstage wearing those, the roar was insane. It was like the whole audience was hugging us and saying, "Let's fucking do this!"

Remember—life can be taken away at any moment. You could be on a slab in a mortuary tomorrow. Make the right choices.

12

Helmets On

BY THE TIME *WE'VE Come for You All* was released in 2003, Anthrax was doing better. Nu-metal was more or less history, and people responded to the new music. I thought it was another great album—but an album that, one more fucking time, suffered from a lack of promotion. It just didn't get the push that it needed, although we worked hard on it.

The upside was that we did a lot of shows on the back of it, more than I thought we would do. I loved being in the band with John Bush, because he's very even-tempered and level-headed. I could always go and have a beer with him and talk about the world. He often stayed at our house, because he's part of our family, like all the guys in Armored Saint. I guess the real outcome of the new album was that we got tight as a band again, and it really set us up to where we went next.

Where *were* we going next? On tour with Motörhead, that's where—and damn, that was always an experience.

I loved everything about Motörhead. We played with them so often that we became tight with their crew as well as with the guys themselves. I would watch their sets from the monitor board at the side because I wanted to see how the magic worked. I'm an eternal bass student, so I always watched how Lemmy picked the strings, and I watched him so closely that I realized he was using two different types of pick.

His onstage sound was fucking ferocious. Those Marshalls were easily the loudest thing on the stage, hands down. I loved every second of it. He and the drummer, Mikkey Dee, would go at each other all the time because Mikkey had Lemmy's amps— basically an entire PA system—blasting away behind him. He'd shout, "You're fucking killing me, man!" and Lemmy would shout back at him, just like Charlie and I do. Every rhythm section does it.

One day I was watching Lemmy play at sound check, and I'm headbanging away, and he sees me standing there. Suddenly he barks, "Come 'ere!" and I go over, scared to death, thinking, "What's going to happen here?" because he's never done this before with any of my band or crew.

Would you believe it, he takes off his bass, puts it on me and says, "Go!" Just like that.

I was so fucking scared, and Lemmy could see that I was afraid and yelled to his tech, "Turn it up!"

Now, if you know the opening scene of *Back to the Future*, where Michael J. Fox stands in front of a massive speaker, that was me right then. I swear to God, when I went up to it and played a big E note, it was exactly like that scene—the speaker reacted so hard that I was pushed back a few steps.

I look over at Lemmy, and of course he's laughing in that evil way. "Hargh, hargh, hargh! Pretty good, eh?"

He knew exactly what he was doing, and also that I couldn't handle it. I sounded nothing like him when I played his bass, so he gives me a pick and says, "Take this. It's one of the picks that I play with." Fuck yes—I still have it now. That was one of my favorite times in my life as a bass player. I feel like a kid in a candy store just talking about it now. He was unique.

I have an equally surreal story about Steve Harris. A few years back, we were touring with Iron Maiden and I was backstage with Michael Kenny, Steve's bass tech. I was looking at Steve's gear, because I am a pathetic nerd when it comes to that stuff, and Michael said, "You wanna try it?"

I said, "Of course!" and man, that was the ride of my life. I was like a kid being handed the football of his hero. Steve's rig is incredibly loud, too. I admire loud bass players, as you can tell.

Still, even though the touring was great around *We've Come for You All*, I was starting to feel that I needed a bit of a break from Anthrax. There were plenty of reasons to stay, of course, including a pretty cool live album that we released in November '04 called *The Greater of Two Evils*. This was easy to do, because it was songs that we knew and loved.

You know, songs change when you play them live for a few years. I played some of the bass parts differently from the way I recorded them. Sting used to say that it's a shame that you don't record songs after you've toured them for a while, because then you know the parts and which ones fit best. That makes a lot of sense. He's a smart man.

It wasn't like I didn't have things outside the band to make me happy. I had a small part on *Law and Order* around this time. I was a big fan of the show, and for once I was around to film it. I had an agent who would suggest me to casting directors on movies, TV shows, and plays, and she would call me when I was home and I'd audition, but it was always difficult for me to sign up for the role—assuming I got through the audition—because I might not be available to play parts two months after I tried out for them.

Anthrax always came first, so they'd say, "Is Frank available?" and my agent would often have to say, "Guess what, Frank's gonna be in fucking Zimbabwe when you're shooting." You could hear the disappointment in my agent's voice. But with *Law and Order* I happened to be available to play a small part in the opening scene, so I went in and read for it and then yes, I was actually going to be home to play the part. I was Jimmy the Rocker, a guy who had four or five lines. Easy stuff, and it was filmed in New York City, so I could get there with no trouble.

Even so, by the spring of 2004, I was unhappy with Anthrax. We needed a break from each other—specifically between me on one side, and Charlie and Scott on the other. We were disagreeing a lot. Musically, we saw things differently. Everybody wanted more of a say when it came to the songwriting, and I was fed up with it. They got tired of fighting about it, I got tired of fighting about it. I felt like I'd hit a wall because I didn't feel I had enough say as an artist.

On top of that, we were also feeling a lot of fatigue because of the way the music business was going at the time. This was starting to affect my health, and I was beginning to suffer from a lot of anxiety. I couldn't breathe because my emotions were so extreme; I felt like I was suffocating, and I think they did, too. I knew I had to get away from the band so I could take a break and breathe for a while.

I remember the exact moment when I realized that I couldn't do it anymore. On that day, tempers had been lost and voices were raised, and I went home. I asked management to issue a statement, and so did Scott and Charlie, and that was it. Both sides knew that we needed to separate. It wasn't like I was fired; it wasn't like I quit. We just needed some space.

It was both easy and difficult to make that decision to walk away. It was easy because everybody needed it to happen—not just me, but Charlie and Scott, too. It was good for all of us to take some time apart. They would be happy if I took off for a while, and I needed time to clear my head.

This needed to happen. I needed to air out my thoughts, and so did they, and it was good for the band. At the same time, it was hard because I was letting go of my security, not just financially but mentally. It felt like a very dangerous place to be in, but that's the tightrope I like to walk in life, if that makes sense. It was scary and exhilarating at the same time because I had no idea what was next.

The big picture is that when you're in a long relationship with anyone—in my case, a twenty-year relationship with the other guys, at that point—you need a break from each other. That's really what the cause of it all was, not anything else.

I sat down in my house and asked myself what I was going to do now. I didn't have anything coming up, or even on the horizon. Maybe I would have to leave the music business, I thought. I really had no idea. Fortunately, I had saved my pennies for a long time, and my wife has a great job, so we weren't going to have any financial worries for a while.

For two weeks I did nothing, which was weird for me because I can't lay around all day; my work ethic is too strong. But then I got a call from my friend John Tempesta. He said, "Hey, I'm with Helmet—come out and jam!" Helmet were looking for a bass player at the time, and John had mentioned me to the bandleader, Page Hamilton.

Now, I love Helmet, and the more John talked, the more it made sense. I knew I wanted to do more with music, and I knew that Helmet were bass-oriented, and I also knew that I would be playing bass with a pick, which would be an interesting change from the fingerstyle playing I'd done before. Suddenly the thought came to me: "Of course you should do this!"

So I flew to LA and met Johnny—who is the best roommate ever, because he cooks and cleans and does everything; he's like Felix Ungar from *The Odd Couple*—and we jammed the songs with the band. It was fucking awesome. I learned thirty-seven songs for that jam. Page started with ten or eleven, but then kept adding more and more.

I was on a salary rather than being a member, which was great, because I played the bass and got paid and didn't have to worry about anything else. I loved the challenge of playing with other people, too.

I likened Anthrax to my first girlfriend whom I'd been with forever, and now Helmet was a chance to be with someone new. They were totally professional, and Page and their guitarist Chris Traynor were so great to play with.

It was a great mix of personalities, and I loved the experience of playing bass differently. The songs on their recent album *Size Matters* were fun to play, and the history of Helmet was really interesting to explore.

We went on tour, and you want to talk about partying? Holy shit, we were on a tear when it came to drinking. Johnny and I really went for it. It was like we were back in high school. I remember we played an 11:00 a.m. show at that year's South By Southwest festival, and he and I were hammered the night before—and we were still pretty messed up the following morning.

When I woke up, I had to get the hair of the dog going before the show. It was coffee and beer that morning, just to get leveled out—and the show was killer. We played the SnoCore tour, too, with a totally different audience for me. The fans couldn't have been more welcoming; to this day, I want to thank all the Helmet fans for welcoming me into their family. And what was also great was that Anthrax fans came to the show, too, to see what it was like. There was really great, positive feedback.

I loved that time of my life. It was scary in parts, but very beneficial for me, because it let me know that I could detach the umbilical cord and that I could do this on my own if I had to. I missed my friends in Anthrax, of course, but I still had a lot of fun. If Helmet hadn't come along, I probably would have put the word out that I was looking for a band, or maybe I would have gone back to school to study something creative. I was glad that Helmet happened, though, because I had the time of my life.

Meanwhile Anthrax had Joey Vera from Armored Saint playing bass with them, which was great because he's such a close friend of mine. I went to see them play in LA, which was surreal. I went backstage and gave them all hugs, because I just didn't want anybody to feel weird—I'm not that guy.

Was it uncomfortable? It was when I first walked in, of course, because I thought people might say, "What the hell's he doing here?" and the fans might say, "Is Frank back?" and I didn't want to confuse them. I just wanted to say hello to everybody, just to break the ice. Maybe everybody felt a bit weird at first, but after we started talking, it was like nothing had passed between us.

There was a great vibe backstage, and afterward I went upstairs and watched the show from my seat, and it was like watching a surreal dream. It was the first time I'd seen Anthrax live. I say in all honesty that it was fun to see what a great band they were, whether I was in it or not. Everybody was at the top of their game.

Before we move on from that period of my life, I have to revisit another tragedy: the death of my friend Dimebag, who was murdered on December 8, 2004. As you probably know if you're a fan of Anthrax, or just from reading the insane stories about him in this book, Dimebag was like the sixth member of Anthrax, hands down. He was family, and he was deeply entrenched in what we did.

He played guitar solos on *Stomp 442* ("King Size" and "Riding Shotgun"), *Volume 8* ("Inside Out" and "Born Again Idiot"), and *We've Come for You All* ("Cadillac Rock Box" and "Strap It On"), and like all the best solos, they were like songs within the songs. The way he played them was all heart, and we were blessed to have him on our songs. I remember we just called him up and said, "Would you do this?" and it was done, without a thought. That's just one reason why his death hit everybody in Anthrax so hard.

I heard about it when I was on tour with Helmet in Germany. Right before our sound check, Johnny told me that Dimebag had been shot and killed in Columbus, Ohio. I didn't believe him and said, "Get the fuck outta here," but then we started hearing it from other people, and then it came on CNN. The tears came then, from us all.

I felt so fucking disconnected because I wasn't there. I thought we should cancel the show and fly home, but of course that wasn't possible. I was a fucking mess. Going onstage was the hardest thing ever, because I didn't know where my center was. Page announced onstage that we had lost our friend, and you could see people in the crowd breaking down in tears.

I couldn't put any of this into words, so I borrowed a drill from a guy backstage and carved "RIP Dimebag" into the bass I played that night. My tears went into the letters I was carving out. It was the only way I felt I could connect with him.

I felt for Vinnie, too, because I'd been through the same thing— my younger brother had been murdered, too. The difference was that it didn't happen right in front of me, as it had to Vinnie, and I couldn't even imagine what that would be like. Our friendship became deeper because of it because there was an understanding and respect that we shared that no one else had whom we knew.

We often talked about it, just him and me, with no one else around. We understood that it could not be understood. We settled on the fact that we would never understand why it happened. We only knew that we had to live on and do what we did, for their spirit. Not their spirit in a religious sense: their spirit in the sense of who they were. Our brothers would have wanted us to move on and get to the next level. We carried ourselves for our brothers, and it's important to move forward. They'll always be with us.

Like I said earlier, it's a choice: you can choose to stay in the misery, or you can choose to move on. Vinnie chose to move on, and he did it in a great way. His life was a party, no matter what, and I always loved that about him. Add Dimebag to that equation and you've got a gift from God—musically and spiritually. They made you feel better about your life when you were with them.

Vinnie himself died in 2018. The last time I saw him was in Vegas, where he lived, and he came to our show—big, beautiful Vinnie, the guy that I loved. We played blackjack and he was the friendly, larger-than-life character that he always was. We drank Black Tooth Grins in Dimebag's honor, and then the party was on. Man, we took a beating at that blackjack table, and we had a great, great time. Vinnie taught me to enjoy the moment, and that's what I did.

I can't believe that it's never going to happen again—that I'll never hang out with the Abbott brothers again. That hurts.

•••

ON MARCH 24, 2005, Anthrax announced that the *Among the Living* lineup was reforming for a bunch of live dates. That meant that Scott and Charlie would be rejoined by three returning musicians— Joey Belladonna, Dan Spitz, and me.

What had happened was that our manager Mike Monterulo had asked me if I'd take a meeting with the other guys to discuss some options. He's my best friend, so I said yes, although I was having so much fun in Helmet. That gig was ongoing, with touring lined up, and I loved the guys and we were having a great time.

Every member of Helmet was a top-notch musician and they were great people, so there were solid reasons to stay with them—but there was a still greater reason to come back to Anthrax, which was that I felt as if something wasn't finished.

At first I was like, "Ah, I don't know, man. I'm having a great time here," but it became obvious that the reunion needed to be done. I guess I didn't want my time in Anthrax to end the way it had in 2004, in bitterness and mutual exhaustion. There was more to give with Anthrax, which had always been my first love and always will be.

There was unfinished business there, and I think we all felt that, creatively. I also think we all learned a little bit more about each other from being apart. We realized that we needed each other to make Anthrax work, regardless of the egos in the band, including mine. We all knew that we worked better together than apart.

I live every day with the understanding that you have one life, and that it's a fucking short one, so I knew it would be better to be all together, having fun, and seeing the reaction from the fans, because I knew a lot of people wanted to see it. People were asking me about the reunion even when I was in Helmet because the rumors were out there. I just said, "I don't know because I haven't talked to anybody yet."

Scott, Charlie, and I had some very healthy conversations about being heard, and about being united. They understood what my problems had been before, and since then, it's been great between us. There are flare-ups, sure, but I think this music needs them because Anthrax needs to sound intense and fresh, and maybe the intensity and the freshness come from the quarreling. I want that spontaneity in the music.

I didn't know if the reunion was going to end after this tour, or if we would go on to do more creative stuff afterward. I had no idea. I hoped that things would work out, because I love the band and I'm proud of what we started. Anthrax is the story of my life, and this was another chapter. I always look at the big picture, and I'm adventurous, so I want to see what's next.

The time apart was important. I cherish that time in Helmet, I honestly do. I understand how it goes in bands; egos get in the way. That is inevitable, because you start the band as equals when you're kids, and over time one or two or three of you get a taste of notoriety, and it becomes addictive, like a vampire feels about blood.

If you don't keep that initial equality, and a power struggle develops, you won't see that band survive, especially if they're strong-minded individuals. You have to be smart enough to talk it out and get on the same playing field. Bands break up when that doesn't happen, because it's the easiest thing in the world to break up—and the hardest thing in the world to stay together.

I knew that everything would be done right when I rejoined. I hadn't quit; it was a mutual separation, or a sabbatical, or even a vacation if you like. All of those words apply. I'll be honest here: I knew there would be a call back to Anthrax while I was in Helmet. I really felt it, whether they thought about it or not. Cooler heads would prevail— we all just needed that space for the health of the band.

Now that I look back, I know that I was still feeling a lot of anger about Anthony's death when I left Anthrax for that year. The therapists tell me, "You just have to learn how to deal with it," which isn't helpful because the void is always there. Therapy does help me to see the big picture more, I guess.

I always ask myself, "What am I doing next?" because as I've said before, life is so fucking short. Any time I need to be reminded of that fact, and I hate to remind you of it because it's so horrible, I think of Anthony's sneakers sticking out from the blanket that covered his body.

The other thing that Anthony's death did for me was to change my reactions to other people's bullshit. I can tolerate a certain amount of it, and beyond that point I'll just move on. I won't even say "Go fuck yourself" to someone who's playing me. I'll just leave. I don't think I'm superior to anyone, but you can't bullshit a bullshitter, right? I've been through enough of it by now, so I won't even call you out on it. I'll just move on. It's the right, healthy thing to do.

I readily admit that I have a temper, but I've worked hard to suppress it and deal with it. I meditate, I do yoga. I literally have to do these things. Most importantly, I think before I react, which comes with age and experience. It's taken a lot of therapy to get to this point, because I'm a fucked-up individual, I really am. I'm trying to figure it all out, still to this day.

I laugh a lot when I think how fucked up I am, for whatever reason that is. I'm just built like this. I don't like the rage in me, although it also fuels me. I just deal with it with the tools that I have.

So we got back together, and we hit the road—hard. We played over 140 shows from April 2005 through October 2006, including the Download Festival, Gigantour, and shows in Australia and Japan. I enjoyed the reunion dates. I thought of them as a renewal for us, and it was nice playing with everybody again.

Sure, everybody has their personalities, and their traits come out just like mine do, and some of us butted heads from time to time. A lot of the arguments are really funny and I love them, with all these stupid phrases that come out of your mouth.

I know the guys in Anthrax as well as I know my own family, and they know me, too. And what's more dysfunctional, and at the same time as comforting, as your family?

13
Brandon

O NE DAY IN SEPTEMBER 2005, Teresa wrote me a note. I picked it up and read it.

It said, "You're going to be a daddy."

I couldn't believe it. I went through a huge wave of emotions, standing right there, as any dad or mom reading this will know. It was like a punch in the face, like, "Oh, my God!" The first thing you say is, "Am I ready for this? This is real!" Then the joy comes, and you cry with happiness, and then your family has all that joy when you tell them.

As Italian families do, my family would always ask me and Teresa when we were going to have kids, right while we were sitting at the dinner table. I would always say, "I don't know. We're not ready," although we were trying for a baby at the time. So, the next time we were there, which was around Christmas, I stood up and said, "I have an announcement," and then shouted, "We're having a baby!" Everybody roared and started hugging and kissing us. It was so great.

I always thought, or at least hoped, that I'd be a great dad, because I worked hard to do it the right way. But I had to be sure about that, so I waited until I knew it for a fact before we started trying for a baby. I was away with Anthrax a lot, of course, but maybe I used that as an excuse to keep waiting, just like I did when I took forever to propose to Teresa. One more time, I just wanted to make sure that I would do it right, because I cannot permit myself to screw it up.

My fear was, and still is, that I would pass the damage I had suffered from my childhood on to my son or daughter. I wanted to clear all that out and be ready for it. All the good things that I had seen in my uncles, and the other great dads that I've come to know over the years, I wanted to give to my child. I'm a big fan of a dad who loves his child and shows him or her the way. I'll always befriend those people.

I knew I'd be forty when Brandon was born, which isn't young for a first-time dad, but it's not super old, either. What's more important is the mom's age, and believe me, when she's pregnant and the doctor starts talking to you about chromosomes and all that scary stuff, suddenly you realize how important her age is.

My wife is four years younger than me, fortunately, but that chromosomes conversation still scared the shit out of me. I remember my fucking heart pounding as this lady was telling us how careful we needed to be. I was thinking, *"Now* you tell us?" I was really worried about that from that point on.

I made sure that I would be home from tour for a couple of weeks around the due date, and the guys in the band were cool about that. Charlie had his daughter Mia four months before, so they understood how important it was.

On the big day, which was May 19, 2006, Teresa had a very hard delivery. I wanted them to do an emergency C-section, and I was saying to this one doctor, "What are you doing? Come on! Let's go!" and they finally pulled her out for the C-section.

I was looking at my wife going through this, and I could feel my world crumbling. At that point, I passed out. Anybody reading this who is a dad will understand why. One minute I was standing there, the next minute two nurses took me into the bathroom, sat me down, and gave me some apple juice. I did recover, fortunately, so I was able to see my son being born.

Of course, when my wife hears me tell this story, she laughs her ass off and says, "Oh, poor Frank, did you faint? Did your blood sugar go down? Oh, that's too bad."

Shit. Women really are stronger than men. It's true.

After that experience, and thinking about my mom going through it five times, we thought, "You know what? Maybe this is a sign that we're good with one child. He's healthy, thank God. Let's not tempt fate." It was a good decision for us. One and done, as they say.

Being a parent is a great part of life. It's the thing that drives me most, as well as being a good husband. For all the reasons you know about because you've read this book, it means everything to me to be a part of a family that's not going to be divided, and to keep that unit going.

Of course, I worry my ass off all the time. I never stop worrying. No dad ever does if he cares about doing it right. In my case, I mostly worry about being on tour so much that I'll miss out on big portions of my son's life. One good thing about Anthrax is that we get to pick and choose our tours these days, but it's still tough.

Luckily, my wife is the best of the best. Picking a strong woman to be my wife is easily the smartest thing I've ever done. Without her, I'd just be stupid Frankie being a dick.

Teresa was bedridden for a little while after Brandon was born, so I had to step up. I'm an amazing diaper changer because of that time in our lives. I could get one out right now and do it in two seconds. I got good at the bath times, and feeding, and all that stuff, too.

Of course, I can't take all the credit for that because I had expert help—I was on the phone 24/7 to my mom and my aunt, saying, "He's got gas! What the fuck do I do here?" But I loved being a hands-on dad in that very early part of Brandon's life.

Our family doctor was a huge help, too: he had been our doctor for three generations of the Benante and Bello families, and was very old-school, telling me, "No, don't do that. Do this!" if I had a question. He's in his eighties and I still travel down to the Bronx to see him.

So, now the task ahead of me was to lay the ghost of my own absent father to rest. How did I do this?

First, I assessed my own faults, because there was no way I was passing them on to Brandon. I used to react to problems quickly and sometimes angrily, so right off the bat, I had to make sure that if I wasn't sure about something, I was going to think it out rather than react. That way I would make sure I knew it was the right way to go.

Next, I would seek help. If I wasn't sure about something, I would bounce it off my wife before I made a dad move. I need to check myself, and the bottom line is that we're raising our son together, so if my insecurity is fucking up my mind, I'll check my decisions with her. She'll give me the yea or nay, which is great because it's a security blanket that stops anything from my past affecting his life.

Discipline is important, so I'll raise my voice if I have to, but hitting is absolutely out of the question. I see other parents do that, but it doesn't make sense to me. Raising your voice should be enough, or even just a look. I learned that from my mother, because she had a great look that clearly said, "You're fucking up!" That's better than any kind of physical punishment.

I'll always try to talk through any problem of that kind. I'll say, "This is why this is wrong." I'll remove Brandon's iPad or his video games if I really have to, which sometimes works and sometimes doesn't. But you know what, I beat the shit out of myself mentally every time that happens. I'm horrible at forgiving myself because I have a lot of scars.

I'm always asking myself, "Did you go too far? Did you go far enough?" That's where my wife comes in, because I can ask her what she thinks. We're a good team that way. I'm not Mr. Dad of the Year, I'm just trying to get through it as best I can.

As a parent, ask yourself what you want for your kid. Personally, I want to raise a good adult who doesn't feel the way I feel or bear any of the scars that I bear. That means everything to me, so I want to create a good, nurturing environment for him. I want him to be strong and to think things through logically. It's an evil world out there, so I want him to be schooled and prepared for it. All this stuff is interesting and scary at the same time.

My philosophy is "go where the love is." I think that's important. That will make you grow. If I can teach Brandon anything in life, that's what it would be. Go where you love and where you are loved. I yearned for that myself for a long time, and it means a lot to me to be in a place where there is love, in my family as well as in my band.

When you see us play, it's all for one. We play with as much energy as we can, and we leave it all on the stage. Sometimes you suck, or you have a bad audience. Every performer has that sometimes. It happens, and you try to pull through it. You get through it and you thank God there's a show the next night, or the night after that, to make up for it. A lot of that is just like the life of a family.

Brandon is proud of me, which means so much to me—more than he'll ever know, until he becomes a dad himself. Maybe even then he won't get it, because he didn't lack a father's love in his life when he was growing up, like I did.

What's funny, but also so gratifying, is that some of his friends at school are Anthrax fans, which gives me a kick. And guess what? He even looks like a young me now, with the long hair and the chain wallet and the boots. That makes me feel so great.

Every day that I wake up to being a good dad, with the chance to be a better dad by enriching my son's life a little, is a day that takes away from the bullshit I suffered. It's a little check mark off the shit I went through. That's my quest, and my job, and my drive, and the truth.

I could always improve as a father, of course. I hope I'm 90 percent there, and I'm proud of that, but I could learn more about helping Brandon to be motivated without being too direct, and I could listen more instead of being overbearing. Listening is a big deal, too, especially when you don't talk.

I'm also working on listening to the music that he loves, which I think is important. He got me into Billie Eilish, whose songs I think are incredible. It's so good to be humbled like that rather than thinking of myself as the guy who knows everything and has to teach my child everything.

I'll try to throw suggestions of music in for him to listen to, of course, just to spice up what he likes, but it's already an outlet for him. I'm so glad about that, because when the pressure valve of life is really tightened up, you can use music to release it.

I think it's great when parents are smart enough to understand what their kids are going through, because we often don't take the time to put ourselves in their position. I sometimes find myself saying to Brandon, "This has to get done, and it has to get done now," and I have to check myself and remember ,"This kid's under a lot of pressure right now, so pull it back." In that situation, I like to take him out of the house and just walk and talk, so there's no pressure on him.

As you know by now, I'm a confronter. If I have a problem with you, I'll say it to your face, so if I sense that Brandon has any kind of problem, I'll immediately say to him, "So what's going on?" and if I can't get through, then I have to bring in the specialist—his mom. They'll go off and have a great talk without me, which I like, because the balance is important.

They have their relationship; he and I have our relationship; Teresa and I have our relationship; and the three of us have our whole-family, triangular relationship, all of which are essential. I guess I'm the disciplinarian, obviously not in a physical way because of all the things we've discussed so far in this book, but in the sense that I'm watching over him to make sure he's on the right track. People have to be held accountable for what they do in life— not just schoolwork while you're a kid, but everything that you do as an adult—and he needs to understand that.

What about teaching him about money? Being a dad has made me reevaluate my own background in that sense. The bottom line is that I had to work for any money that I had when I was a kid.

Poverty made me feel an emptiness in my stomach. I still remember that feeling very clearly, and I feel the need to avoid it as strongly now as I did then. That is the essence of my work ethic, and I'll make a living in any way I can to avoid that. I don't think anybody in life should feel like that, because it's a shitty place to be. I completely relate to poverty when I see it because I understand it in its many different forms. My heart goes out to anyone who suffers from it.

Now, here's a question for you clever people: what happens to a kid's motivation to work hard if they don't have the experience of having lacked something they wanted when they're young? It's an important question. We're working on that right now. Let me know if you come up with an answer.

Brandon is curious about my background, which I'm glad about because it means I can hand him what I've learned, from a situation where there was no dad and no money. It helps him to understand that he's lucky because Teresa and I work so he's never without, within reason of course. Of course, I want him to enjoy a childhood full of love and our presence and financial security, but at the same time I want him to understand that hard work was what got us into that fortunate situation. People have to work for what they want.

Another thing that I try to work on is not spoiling him. My wife sees me doing this, and she points out that I'm trying to make up for my own upbringing. She's right: that's exactly what I'm doing, although it's not conscious on my part. I have to catch myself, which means I have a constant battle going on in my head.

Still, I always try to see the big picture, and I suggest that everybody does this. I acknowledge and agree that I'm a better father, and a harder worker, than I would have been if I hadn't gone through those emotional and financial hardships when I was a kid.

I'm very, very happy being a dad to my son. It's an amazing feeling. In my band, we have a bunch of great dads. This is our main focus now, our kids. Being a dad made me grow up, because you have to if you want to do it correctly.

Always ask yourself what your strengths and weaknesses are as a parent. Personally, I try to help Brandon in every aspect of his life. I don't want there to be any kind of insecurities in his mind, and I want to make sure that he has everything I didn't. That's the bottom line, as I see it, and I think every good parent wants that for their children.

At the same time, I don't want to spoil him too much to where he's not prepared for the world. I think a sense of entitlement is definitely not useful: I want him to work, I want him to learn, and

I want him to have the tools he'll need to survive in this ridiculous, crazy, scary world, and that's my main objective. I think that's the real job of a parent. If I make it long enough, I will be a good grandfather, too, because family will be everything then, just as it is now.

For the most part, I think I'm achieving those goals as a dad, but at the same time, I still have a lot to learn. For example, I could definitely be more patient. My wife tells me that, and I agree with her, so I've been working specifically on my patience. I have to remember that he's his own person. He's not me. I have to remember that and let him grow.

I don't want to be the overbearing father. I'm very, very cautious about that. We have to be disciplinary, but we can't go overboard. I've said three times already that discipline is never physical in my family, because I have to make that crystal clear, but it's not verbal either. Words hurt, and I'm conscious of that.

•••

DOES BEING IN A metal band give me extra perspective on being a father? You're damn right it does.

Think about it. Metalheads have a club, as we know—an inclusive one that welcomes you in, even if you're an outsider. You get to wear the club uniform and to feel the belonging of being a member. With that sense of belonging comes self-esteem, and with self-esteem comes the strength to deal with life and what it can—and will—throw at you.

14

Buckling Up

YOU KNOW, ANTHRAX REALLY wasn't doing great business around 2008 or 2009, and sometimes I needed to remind myself why the heck we persisted. After the reunion, the five original Anthrax members all had the idea of doing an album together, although it wasn't openly discussed if I recall correctly. Scott, Charlie, and I wrote some great music together at this point, but it stayed on the back burner because we were never sure who was going to sing them.

As you can read elsewhere, we looked at a couple of different singers around this time, one of whom was Corey Taylor of Slipknot, whom we love. Creatively, that would have been incredible, but the powers that be stopped it from happening. He's a fan of ours and we're fans of his, and we all gelled so well, with so much mutual respect, and to hear our music with his voice would have been amazing.

I once jammed with Corey at a family member's wedding. He called me up and told me that he needed a bass player in Vegas. It was him, his guitar player, and his drummer, and he asked if I'd come out. I said, "Just get me a flight!" and went out there. We put together twenty-something songs and it was fucking great, with all the eighties pop stuff you can think of. Then he came over to

New York for a book event and asked me to go jam with him at Irving Plaza. We did some acoustic songs and harmonized vocals, and it was great. Corey rules.

I really wanted to work with Corey, but it just didn't happen. The way I look at it, though, the whole thing worked out great because Joey Belladonna came back into play. Everything happens for a reason; you get older and you see that. It's the old cliché, but it's true.

John Bush rejoined us for some cool shows—the Sonisphere Festival in England in the summer of 2009, and Soundwave dates in Australia in early 2010. He's a great friend to this day. John is all about his kids and his family. He's practical and knowledgeable, and he's all heart, all the time, in every way. We had our drunken nights together, and they were some of the most fun times I've had in my life, but we've also had heart-to-heart moments. He stayed at my house for a long period of time while we were working on an album, and he became family. We hung out, laughed, watched TV, drank—just normal family stuff that is so important.

John also has a passion and a hunger and a drive to get his music out, and he also has a real open ear to what makes a song or a vocal better. He'd say, "You gotta take this vocal because it's too high for me," when most singers would insist on doing all the vocals. He's unselfish like that, and one of the good guys. We were very lucky to have him in our band.

From 2007 to 2009, we played shows, of course, but we didn't do many long tours. We had our issues with various singers, and who knows, maybe people were listening to different music back then.

It took a much bigger band to kick us in the ass and make us hungry again.

•••

From the instant we heard that Metallica had invited us to be part of their Big Four live shows alongside Megadeth and Slayer in Europe in 2010, we thought it was a fantastic idea. Metallica being arguably the biggest band in the world meant that it would be a chance for everybody to see what we were capable of. It was so obvious that it was something that we needed to do that it became our mission.

What *wasn't* so obvious at first was that the Big Four shows were going to completely rejuvenate Anthrax's career—and I mean that literally. Those shows gave us new life, and we've never looked back. Joey came back into the band and he's never left, even though the Big Four shows are many years in the rearview mirror as you read this.

What's incredible is that Metallica didn't need to do this. They could easily sell out those huge stadiums on their own. That's why I'll always tip my hat and say thank you to them. The biggest guy on the block doesn't need to do this stuff, but he does it because it's a cool thing to do. They deserve total respect for that.

These shows were going to be the biggest celebration of our lives and our entire journey up to that point. I was just hoping that the whole thing wouldn't fall apart because of the different personalities that there are in the Big Four. I was very worried that they weren't going to come together and realize how special this was. Luckily, it seems that everyone got that message.

The first run of shows was booked from June 16 to June 27, and started in Warsaw, Poland, before running through Switzerland, the Czech Republic, Bulgaria, Greece, Romania, and Turkey. When our plane landed in Warsaw the day before the first show, I wasn't even sure where I was: I got in the van and said, "Where are we going?"

The answer was that we were going out to dinner at a cool restaurant in Warsaw with Metallica, Slayer, and Megadeth, not something I'd ever expected to happen in this lifetime. Of course, Metallica made it very comfortable for everyone, as they always do, and I'll never forget it.

Even though these guys were all my friends, I was a little intimidated at the thought of going in there because I didn't know what the atmosphere was going to be like with all these people together. But I didn't need to be concerned because there was no management and no assistants, just the bands.

It was just the seventeen musicians in Metallica, Slayer, Megadeth, and Anthrax, and that suited me because I like to go up to people and say hi so they don't feel uncomfortable. We walked in and I saw Kirk, then I went up and had a big hug with James, and so it went on: it felt like taking the armor off. They were so smart for doing that.

I noticed that the Metallica guys made a point of sitting with different people, because we were all at different tables, with each band split across the tables—that was a clever way of doing it. It really felt like a celebration, and as I left I realized that this tour was going to have a fucking great vibe.

I couldn't wait to see what the shows were gonna bring. What was Metallica's set list? What was Slayer's set list? What was Megadeth's set list? I was totally excited. I knew everybody was going to step up and bring it, because everybody *had* to bring it. It was like going back to the start of it all, and I loved the fact that we could all catch up before we went out and raged on this thing that we'd all built together. It was such a beautiful atmosphere, and I couldn't wait to get started.

On the day of the first show, it felt like it took forever to get to the venue, an old airfield outside Warsaw, and the anticipation was huge because we didn't know what kind of event it was going to be or what the backstage was. Walking into the event, we knew immediately that it was special.

It was massive. We'd all come from these same small clubs, and now we were on this huge piece of land that people were gonna fill up. All the way up, so that we couldn't see the end of the crowd.

I remember the roar from the crowd from before we even went onstage. I was like, "Oh, my God!" It was insane. When I see film clips of that event, I relive it and get the adrenaline surge all over again. The stage was so far from the people, and yet we were so close—right in each other's faces, because we were so connected.

And I got to play the famous bass riff in "Heaven and Hell," the Black Sabbath song that we played in honor of Ronnie James Dio, who had died exactly one month before that Warsaw show. His passing had hit us all hard in the metal community. Joey was close with Ronnie, as I mentioned before, and when he sang that song, he put a little extra into it out of respect, because the two of them used to talk about their art—two great singers that they were.

When you have that energy in your performance, you know it's gonna sound right, and then when we saw the crowd reacting the way they did, it gave us a huge feeling of warmth and excitement. I felt that Ronnie would have been so proud of that. No one expected it from us, and I just kept saying to myself, "Dig into this song. Dig into it."

At the Sofia show, which was recorded for a DVD, there was that extra pressure with the show that comes with being filmed, because I worry about camera operators coming onstage. We have a pretty active show, and I don't want it to be ruined for people who paid to see it, which is very important. You might turn around fast and knock your bass out of tune, or break your nose, on a camera that's right behind you. Still, it worked out fine. I worry too much, don't I?

On the group encore of "Am I Evil?" I stood next to James, and it was just so much fun to jam with him. He looked over and gave me that "let's headbang" look, so I went over and we did exactly that, which took me right back to the early days of our careers. We'd done this before, in the eighties.

Everyone was hugging each other onstage. I loved seeing Mustaine do that, especially. You can see me on the DVD or YouTube, really enjoying the moment. I was on cloud nine: you're looking at the fifteen-year-old Frank Bello onstage, right there, being so thankful and living out my fantasy in front of all those people. I watch that footage now and I see how big of a deal that was.

Our next album, *Worship Music*, had been slowly taking shape since 2008, but now that Joey was back on board, he recorded his vocals and it was scheduled for release in September 2011. In the months leading up to it, we played in the Philippines and then at more Big Four shows, the first one at Indio, California, and then five more in Germany, Italy, the famous Knebworth House in England, and then a final European show in France—before the biggest one of all from Anthrax's point of view: Yankee Stadium, in New York, on September 14.

You can imagine what it meant to Anthrax to sign off this incredible event in our hometown. And not just to us, either: the borough president of the area where Charlie and I grew up actually made September 14 Anthrax Day. They came and presented us with this award, and the Hard Rock Cafe in the stadium still has our signed jerseys up on the wall.

Playing Yankee Stadium was so huge for us. The home fans were there for us. I grew up ten minutes from the stadium, and I was a die-hard Yankees fan, too, so getting to play on that stage was insane for many different reasons. Who gets to do that? Seriously?

What makes me happy, but breaks my heart at the same time, was that it was the last Anthrax show that my grandmother got to see. We had a box for her and my aunts, although I couldn't get up there to say hello before the show, and they had left already by the time I got up there. I did see her in the parking lot, though, and I gave her a big hug and a kiss.

I asked her, "Did you enjoy the show?"

"That was great. I loved it."

I remember how much Tina enjoyed the show, and it was huge for me that she got to see the most important gig in our history before she passed away. I see that show as a thank you to her. She nurtured me and Charlie and made this possible, and I wanted her to know that this wouldn't have happened without her.

She made it all possible for us, because she let us know that it was okay for us to follow our passion, and I do the same: I watch over my son and protect him, but I don't suppress him from doing what he wants to do. It's an important lesson that I learned from her.

When you think about the timeline of events, it was symmetrical: exactly three decades passed between the first time she saw us play in 1981, when Charlie and I were jamming in her house, and 2011, when she saw us play Yankee Stadium. As I sat by myself in that empty stadium for a few minutes that day, I thought about that, and I took the time to be grateful.

I hope that, circumstances being right for everybody, the Big Four shows could happen again sometime. I know Slayer retired, but people can always come out of retirement. I would say to those guys, "What time are we in this life? How many times are we gonna get the opportunity to do this, one more time?"

•••

In 2012, I ACTED in a cool independent film, *Greetings from Tim Buckley*. I played the role of Richard Hell, the real-life punk musician, and it was a role that I did over eight days of work, starting really early each day, so I had to get up around 4:00 a.m. because I had to take two trains to get there.

I'm a die-hard Jeff Buckley fan and so I'm a Tim Buckley fan, too. The film is about Jeff not knowing his dad, Tim, which is interesting because that's also a part of my history. I didn't even realize that until we watched it during the writing of this book. That's a coincidence. It's so strange that I didn't even acknowledge that at the time.

The process was like this. First, I auditioned for the casting director. After that, the director wanted to meet me, but we could never find a time to get together because he was busy doing a million things for the film. Finally, we met and had a great conversation about Richard Hell; I wanted him to know that although I was a musician, I wasn't this rocker guy.

The audition was nerve-racking, I have to say. I didn't know if a big star would come in and get the part that I wanted. When there's any name actor attached to a film, he'll get the role over Frank from Anthrax, because nobody gives a shit about Anthrax in the movie world. So I was very worried about that; it's happened before. You do great reads and then they say, "Oh, we went with the name guy." It's understandable, of course.

Now, when I auditioned for the part, it was for a very famous casting director whose name you've seen in a million credits, so I was intimidated going in to read—but I'll tell you, I knew it inside out because I'd done so much work on him. I was confident doing the read, and I remember doing the callback and meeting one of the actors, whom I knew, who was coming out after reading for the same part.

I asked how it was going and he said, "I think she's already got somebody, because she said he's coming in next." The next guy coming in was me, so that made me feel great. I was pretty psyched about that. The casting director kept asking my agent if I was available, and it worked out.

On the first day of filming, it was totally intimidating, yet again. I remember walking in for the first scene, which was being shot at a church in Manhattan. As you know, I'd done acting work before—*Married...with Children* and all that stuff—but this time I was playing Richard Hell, not Frank Bello from Anthrax. I felt like I had to deliver here, and that I had to work fucking hard, so I really dug in.

I was proud of myself because I got a lot of compliments about my performance. Look, nobody is Robert De Niro, and I'm not pretending to be, but I do work hard. In that situation you break your ass, and the payoff is the acknowledgement that you did a good job and you've left it all on the table. That's what I did with that role.

I had to get to know the producers, who were watchful of their investments and who was cast. I think I was a little outside the box—you know, an actor who was also in this well-known band. They were cautious, but they were very welcoming. The director Dan Algrant was awesome with me because he was open to any ideas I had. We did a couple of rehearsals for scenes and he said, "I like where you're going with this." That was a confidence-builder right off the bat.

Think about what it's like for me to step onstage without a bass guitar. It's scary as hell. Maybe it's a mental deficiency that I have, though, because I love that challenge. I love being scared and pushing myself forward. It's almost like a do-or-die thing— like, "Fuck it! Let's see what happens."

In the case of Richard Hell, I lived the character, and I did a lot of reading to understand his personality. I found him fascinating. I looked into his history and studied how he was in interviews to understand how he talked and stuff like that. You have to play the role as yourself, though—you put it out in your way of portraying it. It can't be how other people would do it.

Anger's always the easiest emotion to go to. I live with a buffet of anger every day of my life, so that's the easiest thing to do. I have my whole history in my mind, so emotions are pretty easy to get out. As you know by now, I'm an emotional person, and so much of my happiest emotions are tied up with the TV and movies I saw as a child.

I'm a seventies kid, and back then my all-time favorite TV show was *The Mary Tyler Moore Show*. First off, the writing was amazing—it was the purest of comedy. It made me laugh my ass off when I was a kid, and it was totally escapist for me. Ted Knight, who was also in *Caddyshack*, is one of the most underrated comedic actors ever in my book, hands down. His timing, his mannerisms, everything he did was for a reason, and unfortunately people don't know enough about him. I wish I would have met him.

I actually did meet Gavin MacLeod, whom you'll know from *The Love Boat*. I went to a horror convention in New Jersey, and the owner is a friend of mine and hooked me up to meet Gavin because I told him I was a huge Mary Tyler Moore fan. I said I'd get a picture with him and leave. So he calls me over to meet Gavin MacLeod, and we sat down and talked about the cast and the crew and Ted Knight.

I was immediately in fanboy mode, sitting there with one of the guys who made me feel happy when I was a kid. He knew how into it I was, and we talked for fifteen minutes, even though there was a line of people waiting to talk to him and they were getting pissed at me. I said, "I'd better get going," and he said, "No, stay a couple more minutes." That was a beautiful moment for me.

There was *M*A*S*H**, too, which I still watch today on MeTV, a specific channel that only has old TV shows. I watch it religiously every night because it's better than anything that's out now, if I'm honest. Quality means a lot. They had impeccable writers and actors. Alan Alda was so far ahead of his time. It had the biggest finale ever, and it could be pretty dark, too—they showed a real side of war while keeping the comedy really sharp.

Never underestimate the emotional depth you can access from watching cartoons, too, no matter how childish they seem. The whole point is that they're childish, if you're looking to tap into a child's emotions. *The Bugs Bunny Show* was huge for me because it was years before *The Simpsons* but it had exactly that kind of sarcasm.

The same goes for the *Looney Tunes* characters Wile E. Coyote and the Road Runner, where the coyote keeps dying, just like Kenny does in *South Park*. Those writers were the best in the world. The Disney films looked beautiful to me, too, but they always left me feeling sad. *Bambi* imprinted on my brain, like it did on the brains of an entire generation of kids my age.

I can't overstate the importance of *The Odd Couple*, too—both the original film from 1968 and the later TV series. I'm an avid fan of the Turner Classic Movies channel, which has the old films, and they had the original movie on recently, so I recorded it and watched it last Christmas with a beer in my hand after everyone else was asleep.

Watching it, I went deeply into the acting. Walter Matthau and Jack Lemmon—that's an entire school of acting, right there. These guys live in those fucking characters. To this day I can find something new in it every time I watch it. I'll say, "Look what he did there. Why is he cutting that piece of chicken that way?" And then they made this great TV version with Jack Klugman and Tony Randall, also great actors, which had a five-year run from 1970. I have those and *The Mary Tyler Moore Show* on my iPad, so if I'm stuck in some hotel room, I'm never alone and I always have comfort. It's home and it's a safe place.

You want to talk about movies? I think I was around eleven or twelve when I first saw *The Godfather*, and I've seen it hundreds of times since then. Not only for the story, but for the acting—I just want to see what they do. You have the best of the best in those first two movies.

The Italian-American movie tradition is appealing to me because I've known stories like that myself, and guys like that in real life. It was a great story and a very clever one, and it became an acting class because all those actors created a living moment. I learned that it's not about the lines, it's what you do and how you live them.

That is entrenched in me from studying acting. I found that wisdom so appealing. It was therapeutic at a time in my life when I hadn't been to therapy yet. When I went into therapy after my brother's death, I found that I had already been doing therapy through acting. As I told you, I was hell-bent on vengeance, and I needed to get my head straight. To alleviate that, I went to therapy, because I didn't want to lose my wife and I didn't want my mom to have a second son dead or to see me go to jail. That's how dark it was. As you know, I still think about that time.

When the idea of acting started to appeal to me, it was because the challenge of living in the moment attracted me—the idea of burying myself in someone else. It felt so cool to create an imaginary person, just like a great song. There are no boundaries in either one, which is why I've always loved the art of acting. You find out a lot about yourself. The shit I've found out about myself through acting, because I went places in my head, has blown my mind.

Looking back at *Greetings From Tim Buckley* right now in 2021, it makes me want to go out and read for parts and audition more.

I like the whole commitment of it all. I like the bouncing off of people, and just learning from other actors. One of the actors in that film was actually a Broadway actress—she literally did her scenes with us during the day, and then went to do a theater show that night. That's how dedicated she was, and for me to be working with that caliber of actors was amazing. It was a great experience.

Again, with all this creative art, you can see that it's all for one, right? Acting is just like jamming in a band. It all serves the song or the play or the movie. Ask yourself what is at the end of it all. What happens then, and what are you left with? Are you left with a scene that works? Whatever you do with that moment is what remains—there are no retakes, it's just you just doing it.

I appreciate the skills of a good director, too. He or she will throw something in that helps you to get your performance right, and that acknowledgement is essential, because I like to listen and learn. I want to learn everything, and I want to learn from other actors, too.

William Sadler was in *Greetings from Tim Buckley* and he was fucking awesome. You'll know him from movies like *The Shawshank Redemption* and *Trespass*, and maybe even the second *Bill & Ted*, where he plays Death. He was so friendly, and in the scenes that we shot when we first started, he would give me tips. He goes, "You know what, let's start it like this," and he would help me with that stuff: we even did a private rehearsal. He was so kind, and he's an experienced actor, so he made it very comfortable for me just by talking.

I don't act to be famous, I do it because I love the art of it. I want to give everything to that character. Whether the movie is a success doesn't matter to me. It genuinely doesn't matter. *Greetings from Tim Buckley* was not going to be a blockbuster, but that's fine. It was an independent film that I really cherished doing, and I hope to do more of them in the future.

They flew us to Toronto for the film festival. The crazy thing is that one of the producers flew me back home in a private plane. It was my first flight in a private aircraft, in all those years with Anthrax, until we flew in Iron Maiden's plane. I was hoping that the flight would be longer, but it was just Toronto from New York. It was absolutely incredible.

I've done dozens, or maybe hundreds, of auditions by now. I even auditioned for *The Sopranos* a couple of times. I would always tie my hair back in a ponytail, in case they didn't like my long hair, although they did cast a guy with a ponytail once, in the character of Furio.

One more time, it's not about being famous—it's about finding out what makes me tick, and that's a lifelong journey. Acting is a tool to get me that. My weaknesses, my triumphs, just being able to write music for myself. Just writing this book is digging up some stuff for me, with lyrics that come easily but from a place of darkness. It's all working itself out.

What else have I done? There was a play called *Cantorial*, which is very foggy because it's way back in the nineties. It wasn't even off-off-off-Broadway—it was in a tiny, corner place. I remember being nervous about starting it, but once I was over the hump I was fine. Then I had two lines in the MTV film *Joe's Apartment*, where I played a stick-up guy. Believe it or not, I had to read for that part.

As a low-budget independent movie, it was exhausting, but that's how you know you're into it, because there's no real money at this level. During the process, with all this dialogue, and all the work I put in to dig into this character, I got excited by it, which is how I knew that acting was for me. This is how you learn—it was a great learning experience. That's why it worked for me. I just wanted to get better, and the way to get better is to work hard.

The headlining name is what gets you through the door, and I'm a nobody in the acting world, so there are a lot of people before me. I'm a competent actor because I put a lot of hard work into it, but names mean everything, and they get your movie made. Casting directors have a network of actors that they like and use, so you have to get through that, too. It's like climbing a mountain, from one tier to the next. That's why people say, "If you're in the movie industry for the long haul, it's a heartbreaker."

I've auditioned for some huge films, and usually I knew there was no chance in hell I'd get the part, because there was already a big name attached to that part. In fact, I wanted the part to go to that actor, but you audition anyway because you want to build a relationship with the casting director. It's all about getting in there and making a relationship, because you might get a two-line bit part that catches the casting director's eye and they say, "That guy's good, let's get him in next time." But you don't stand a chance in hell of getting the big part the first time you go in.

When they call me in for an audition with a casting director, I bust my balls learning the scenes that they want. The monologues, too. You live this scene, and then they look at you and you get a vibe from them whether you've done good or not. It's like a job interview: you get a feeling about how well you came across. Sometimes you'd feel fucking great, and the vibe is good. Sometimes, not so much.

For me, going into a monologue in front of a director and blocking the world out is challenging because you don't know how people are going to react. I put a lot of work into it because I'm a worker and I like digging into a task as much as my ability allows, but I still think, "Suppose they hate this monologue?" just as I might think, "Suppose the audience hates this song?"

Maybe they'll say, "Frank, that was great. I'm looking at your résumé. You're in a band, right?" So straight away you know they think you're not taking this seriously, even though you've worked hard just to study under the teachers you've been with. They'll ask, "Did your agent tell you about the dates of this production?" and that rips your heart out, because there's a tour starting a week before the show starts.

All of a sudden, you're out of the running and that's happened so many times to me. I'm not saying I got every part that I auditioned for, but I got some really good callbacks that I couldn't go to because I wasn't going to be available. But that's life.

In acting, you're stripping yourself down in front of an audience. You're exposing your heart to people. That's scary, but I love it. That's why we're living. What's the worst that could happen? People could judge you negatively, but I can easily live with that. Whatever the feedback is, it will lead you to your next venture.

This was one of my favorite times in my life, just because there was so much happening in a positive way, career-wise. As Gene said in the foreword to this book, we run a race, and the race is called life. I try to run it as fast and as well as I'm able, while I still can.

15
Father, Brother, Son

MY FIRST REAL MUSIC outside of Anthrax was Altitudes & Attitude, a duo with David Ellefson of Megadeth. I love what we've done with that band, and it all started with a series of bass clinics that Hartke, my amp company, asked us to do after the Big Four shows.

David's tone really grabbed me at those shows. I always check out other bass players, because if I hear a cool tone, maybe I can incorporate it into my playing. You always have to have an open mind: don't be locked in. So David was coming out with this killer sound at sound check, and he took me through what he was using on his rig and let me try it. He then hooked me up with Hartke, and those guys have been amazing to me ever since.

I said to the guys at Hartke, "I want to get out and do clinics, because people should know what bass products are good that they can get for a decent price," so David and I went out and did a bunch of them. That's how Altitudes & Attitude got started. He said to me one day at one of these clinics, when we were jamming, "Why don't we write some original songs?"

I had quite a few songs that I'd written, and so did he, so we got Anthrax's producer Jay Ruston on board, and I got rolling with the lyrics. We really wanted to do this project, and we put all our efforts into it. The songs really tie in with the things we've talked about in this book, and they've been therapeutic for me.

One small downside is that some people get weird when they see me playing a guitar rather than a bass, because they feel that I've been taken out of my usual role, but I explain to them—with no disrespect intended—that I've been playing guitar since the very beginning. Of course, if someone cares about a detail as small as that then I take it as a compliment because presumably they're a fan of what I do.

I know that Steve Harris writes songs on bass, and in fact I've asked him how he does it. I understand that you can write a bass line like it goes through the song, of course, but for me, the song flows better when you write it on guitar. You can include major and minor chords, which allows the angst in me to come out way easier. I'll write the chords on the guitar and then right after that, I'll go to the bass.

I loved passing on my knowledge at those Hartke clinics, and a few years later I enjoyed taking part in some Little Kids Rock events for the same reason. The charity asked me to talk to some kids about playing in a band, and I said, "Sure, whatever I can do," and I went to talk to the kids about how important music is.

It was like doing a clinic without doing the clinician stuff, because it was really about passing the spirit of music along. We gave them a bunch of basses, and it felt great to see them play my signature instruments. Again, it was about passing the torch, and that is very, very important for everybody.

Anthrax has been busy touring ever since the Big Four shows, with only one lineup change: that was in 2013, when Rob left to join Volbeat. He got an offer to produce the Volbeat record, and then joined them, which I totally understood.

I'm a Volbeat fan and I'm friends with those guys. We went on tour with them and we had a fucking blast. It was great to see

Rob join them. I was and still am happy for him, because that band is where he belongs. I talk to him all the time because he only lives ten minutes from me.

Rob recommended Jon Donais from Shadows Fall to take his place, and we've been very lucky with that because it was totally seamless. Jon is the most easygoing guy in the world, and a great fucking guitar player.

In 2013, we released a covers EP, *Anthems*, and if anybody knows Anthrax, they know from the B-sides we put out through the years that all we do is jam other people's songs. We're all big Radiohead fans, for example—we had previously covered their song "The Bends." I think that band is underrated, and they don't get enough promotion for the great music they're putting out right now.

The same year we toured with Testament and Death Angel, and we did the Metal Alliance tour with Exodus. I want people to know how great these tours were with those bands, who are some of my best friends in the world. When we tour with these guys, there's such a "home" feeling, from Chuck Billy to Alex Skolnick to Mark Osegueda, all of those guys. We've become like family with them, and they're very good people.

The great thing about these tours is that I'm able to watch the other bands and get off on their performances. I want to see everybody in those shows do well, from the opening band to the middle band to the headliner. I want the crowd to be fucking floored. That's so important—I want everybody to play the greatest show they have ever played so everybody has a great experience.

You know, in the early days we probably would have been competing with those other bands, but over these last couple of years I just want to enjoy it because you realize that it could all be taken away in an instant, just like that. When we're in the moment, I always think to myself, "How fucking lucky are we? How lucky are we to be able to stand on the side and watch our friends play such killer music?"

Our most recent album, *For All Kings*, came out in 2016, and we worked hard on it, because let's face it, these songs are what you have to live with for the next three years. That's the way I look at it in Anthrax—I want to live with the songs—so when we have these arguments about writing, my argument is that I have to fucking live with them for how many hundreds of shows for the next three years. That's why I want to make sure every part is right.

It took five years to release *For All Kings* after *Worship Music*. People ask about that five-year gap, and I totally understand the question because I'm also one of those fans that says, "What the fuck were you doing all that time?" But when you look at our touring schedule and the amount of time that took out of every year, it makes sense.

Anthrax has never been one of those bands that could write records on the road. You've got to make sure that the songs are lived with, and you need to make sure that they're the best of the best. We went out with Lamb Of God, we went out twice with Killswitch Engage, we did tons of touring. We never stopped, and that's all good, because it means the previous album was successful and that a lot of people want to see you play.

With the new album we thought we had lightning in a bottle—we really did—and it turned out that it did cross over the way we needed, and people understood what it was exactly the way we wanted them to. A lot of people used the word "rebirth" to describe it, which was good of them, and we appreciated that they did that—but for me, Anthrax has always been a constant, so it was never a rebirth. As I saw it, we never really went away.

Still, I was excited about this new record, because I was happy that this reunion happened in such a great way. The quality is right there, on the record, and how great is that? You don't have to say anything when the proof is in the pudding. The record spoke for itself, and thankfully, people caught on to it, and I say that humbly, because you don't know which way it's gonna go. Our fans are smart enough to understand that it's all from the heart in our band, and thankfully, they've stayed around all this time.

Okay, here's another good story. We did a South American tour with Iron Maiden...on their own plane. Time to grab another drink and listen up!

First off, imagine me, some guy from the Bronx, being in a band that was opening for Iron Maiden in South America. Maiden has always been, and will always be, one of my favorite bands of all time. Before this tour, we'd played Iron Maiden shows and enjoyed some great, packed-to-capacity tours with them, with a great fanbase. I loved Iron Maiden's fans, a lot of whom became Anthrax fans after they saw us play, which was awesome.

But had we done anything on the scale of this specific tour? Hell no.

When we heard about it, we went nuts. This was a stadium tour—a *stadium* tour!—in South America. Right off the bat, when you hear that, your mind is blown, because you know Iron Maiden is one of the world's biggest bands and that they can sell out stadiums, specifically in South America.

When my manager said those words to me, I started babbling immediately and saying, "No fucking way! You're fucking kidding!" The kid inside me came out at that moment—the kid who met Steve Harris in that pub nearly forty years ago.

And here's the cherry on top: we were going to travel on Maiden's plane, Ed Force One, with them, with their singer Bruce Dickinson flying it. I didn't know whether to scream or shit my pants. Everything you could ever dream of as an Iron Maiden fan was coming true at this moment. I'd had a lot of great times with them before this, and I thanked them for that—but I never thought something like this would ever be possible, just like I never thought Anthrax could ever play Yankee Stadium.

Even after the tour was confirmed, I still couldn't really believe it was happening. All the way down to Monterrey in Mexico, where we were meeting Maiden and getting on their plane, I was predicting that somehow it wasn't going to work out, because it was just too good to be true.

When we arrived in Monterrey and got our first glimpse of Ed Force One, parked on the runway at the airport, we couldn't believe our eyes. I was like, "Is this really going to happen? Are they really going to let us on?" I was like a little kid. It was a huge Boeing 747, and all of our band, our crew, and all our gear went on it.

I was wondering if there would be special zones for everyone, with security and everything, but it was totally relaxed. You'd think they'd have Iron Maiden in the front and keep us in the back, but no. Maiden did have an upstairs room, but the production coordinator, Zeb Minto, who is a friend for life and who has always looked out for Anthrax, gave us all business-class seats and took care of our families and the crew families, too.

Imagine, as you're sipping a beer while reading this in the pub, or at home, or wherever you are, what it's like to be an Iron Maiden fan, traveling like this, on the way to play sold-out stadiums. It doesn't get better than that in this life. I want you to understand how I felt sitting in that seat—and remember what a business-class seat means if you come from a childhood of poverty. No wonder I was scared shitless that this was all going to go away, any second.

I just sat there and tried not to get in the way. I'm friends with Maiden, but I didn't want to take up any of their time because this was their home territory. Steve and Nicko would come up and say,

"How you doing, Frank?" and I'd say, "Great, but I don't want to get in your way." They'd say, "Oh, stop! Enjoy yourself. Have a drink. You had a Trooper yet?"

I remember Steve giving us a case of ice-cold Trooper beer to welcome us to the tour. He knew we were loving every second of this, and he wanted to make sure he got it right. That's class. Iron Maiden know how to do it right, from the manager on down to the crew, whom I'm very close to.

Steve is still showing me how it's done, all these years after he first showed me how it's done in New York in 1982. Gene, too: he never let anything get in the way of his path, and that's very inspirational. You don't need to let things derail you if you have a goal in mind. If I'd gone out on a Friday night when I was a teenager instead of staying in and learning to play a Rush song on bass, it would have derailed me. Why do it?

That same year—how the fuck we got all this stuff done in a single year, I have no idea—we went on tour in North America again, this time with Slayer and Death Angel. We played in Atlanta one night, and because we're all die-hard *Walking Dead* fans, we went out to the set when we were there. We went through the town where they shoot it, we went backstage, we went into the writing room. They couldn't have been nicer to us.

If you're into *The Walking Dead*, you might know that Norman Reedus, the actor who plays Daryl Dixon, is a huge rock and metal fan. We ate and drank with him and had a great fucking day, and then we went back to do our show. It was one of those great days that makes you think, one more time, how fortunate you are to do this.

That night, Norman came to watch the show from the side of the stage. I knew he dabbled in bass, so I was busting his chops before we went on, saying, "Come up and play bass with us tonight!" He said no, although I could see he kinda wanted to say yes.

When the show started, Norman was at the side of the stage, totally getting it, just jamming with himself and getting into the headbanging, so I went over to him, stuck a bass around his neck and said, "Dude, let's do this!" He walked out with me and the crowd went fucking wild, because this super-famous guy had walked onstage with us. He didn't know the songs, but it didn't matter because we were having such a blast. I walked him through some bass parts, and then he took off. What a badass that guy is, and a great fucking actor, too.

Like I said before, I'm a fan who likes to hang out at the side of the stage, too, and when we played on Slayer's final tour in 2019, I was right there every single night. There's a lot of pictures online of me on the side of the stage. You know those guys are all my friends: I love their music and I love the band. And because I know this is not forever, later on in life I want to remember these times. I want to have them in the catalog of my memory and say, "I want to go back to that event, because it was such a fucking great time."

Just saying that to you now unlocks another memory door for me—the times we had on the tour we did with Pantera. Every night, after the Anthrax set, as soon as I dried off from the shower, I was on the side of the stage with a beer in my hand watching them, because I knew how fucking special it was.

I knew it wasn't gonna last, of course, even though you want it to last forever, but I didn't know that it was going to be taken away in the way that it unfortunately was. But I knew how special Pantera was. I was on Rex Brown's side of the stage every night, and when Rex came over, we did a fucking shot. It was our thing, man, and I want people to understand that, which is why I'm talking about how much love I have for it.

I wish you could have been on the side of the stage, next to me, with Pantera fucking rocking out, loving every song, rallying them on, and watching the crowd go absolutely apeshit. Rex would come over and shout, "Let's go!" We'd slam a shot down, and then— holy shit!—Dimebag would come over, and we'd do another one. I was fucking plowed by the end, but I was such a fan that it was important for me to be on the side of the stage. It's where your heart is, and it's the best feeling in the world. I love it.

I'm really not joking when I say that I wish you, my friend reading this right now, could have been there with me. Imagine if you were there, just waiting for the time when Rex got that look in his eye, like "it's on!" and then you knew that the shot was coming. He'd be telling his crew to get this specific guy that they employed just to fucking pour whiskey—they really had a specific guy who did that. And you're thinking, "Can I handle this one? Can I handle one more?" Then the guy comes over and gives you one of these fucking things, which is half a glass of Crown Royal with a little tiny bit of Coke in it.

Those days are gone, which is sad, but it's how life goes. What's important is that you enjoy the good times, and hold onto them in your memory, and learn from them, as I hope this book has made clear along the way.

Me, I'm grateful for everything that happened in the run-up to working on this book: Altitudes & Attitude released an album, *Get It Out*—you think the title might have anything to do with the things I've talked about here?—and Anthrax played the Megacruise in 2019, one of the last things we did before the world shut down for a couple of years.

We've been working on a new album during the pandemic. Who knows, it might be on the way by the time you read this. I've also worked on some cool collaborations. My friend Bill Kelliher from Mastodon asked me if I wanted to be part of a cover of Faith No More's "We Care a Lot," and he told me that Dennis Lyxzén from Refused was singing on it. I was instantly on board because Dennis is a star—he has that kind of energy and a voice that roars. That guy will always bring an audience, wherever he is.

And I love Bill Gould of Faith No More: his bass lines are incredible. The first time I met him, I told him that I was a huge fan. I like the way he thinks bass. His playing is always outside the box, but it's orchestral. He'll take a song and write something that fits so well, in a really tasty way. I try to do the same with my bass parts—to write a line that goes really well with the main melody.

I look around at today's music and I see a lot of amazing, underrated musicians. They're underrated because there's so many of them playing at such a highly technical level. YouTube is saturated with great musicians. I only find out about great musicians when I tour with them, specifically at sound checks that I watch, and if I talk to bass players about their gear, because the rest of the time, life gets in the way.

When I come home from tour, I don't want anything to do with anyone outside my family. I don't want to touch a bass for at least a week, partly because my fingers are raw but also because I need a complete cleansing. I don't want to listen to the latest bass player on YouTube, either. After a while I start to get interested in music again, and I start listening to new bands.

I can't wait to work on new music with Anthrax. I've learned to compromise over the years. They say a good compromise is when no one walks away happy, and Anthrax is right on point with that. But despite the tension of the writing process, the band are my brothers. I've been with them more than with my own family.

Metal was always a rock for me. I could put my headphones on and it would take me away. It was always right there for me, through the hardest times. I'll never forget that, and I hope that people have something like that in their lives that will take them through the ups and downs. It doesn't have to be music, it just has to be anything that they can rely on. If you have something like that, remember how lucky you are.

Metal gives me a lot of energy, too. People have often mentioned that they notice my energy levels onstage, and I thank them for that. It's my thank you to them. Every time I walk onstage, I'm so thankful because I get to live out all of my fantasies. All the things I feel in life, I let them out, and I don't care. It's primal, like the primal scream therapy that Gene mentions in the foreword to this book.

My whole objective is to enable everybody to have a good time. Let's share this energy and get a vibe going. Let's do this thing, the audience and us together, and bring it to the top. That's what it's supposed to be about. See how all of the above is connected with being part of a family?

After nearly forty years together, I look back and think, *Fuck, man. Anthrax has been really good to me, and I want to pay it back.* I love what we've done, and I'm sure there's a lot more to come. There's yet another rebirth to be had. It's about that hunger. Our work ethic is great, and when we get together in the studio, there is no better feeling than when everybody has their shit down and there's no slacking.

Everybody is going to be at the top of their game because everybody cares that much. Nobody's laying back, nobody's thinking, "I'm not into this." Everybody gives a thousand percent. I love that about the personalities of Anthrax, and I love that we still have it after so long.

We still want to push the envelope. I can't wait to see what's next. I don't know what it is yet, and I don't want to know, because I want it to happen naturally without being contrived. We've never been contrived.

I look back at my life, and I realize what a gambling mentality I've had all along. You know what doesn't stand a chance in hell? Joining a band at the age of seventeen, signing to a major label, selling millions of albums, touring the world, and making a forty-plus-year career out of it.

Well, that happened to me—so never give up on an opportunity, because there's always a chance. Why not? I didn't know where the fuck it was going at the time. I just knew I had to do it. The process is everything, and the rest is bullshit. The journey is the whole point.

I never want to say in my life "I should have." Fuck that! Let's do it and see what happens. You know what? I know that if I've done the work and the research, I won't fail.

Regrets? I have none, although I think there are things I could have tried. I sometimes think I should have moved to California when Scott did, around 1990, before I was a husband and a father. I wanted to do it, but my family was here in New York, and I didn't want to leave them because I would have missed out on all those great times.

Not just the big occasions, but the small ones that are so important, like hanging out and drinking coffee with my grandmother on a Sunday morning. I would never have had those times if I'd moved. So I freeze my balls off in New York, and I pay ridiculous taxes, but at the same time I have all these treasured memories. That's more important than an eighty-degree temperature. I'll move to Florida or Nevada when I'm old and withered up. I'll still be youthful in my head.

Am I sad that certain things happened? Yes, and it's okay to be sad. I'm sorry that we didn't have a normal family unit. When my dad took off, we disbanded. None of that is our fault, I'm just sorry that it happened. We rallied around it, and we moved on. Remember, people deal with worse circumstances than that every single day. Thank God I had a loving family, even if it wasn't the standard dad plus mom plus kids, because a lot of people don't have that, and I'm very thankful. That's why family is my foundation, and it always will be.

I want my son to have that foundation, too, and all fathers should know that, if they ever think of cheating or leaving their family. Think about what it does to your children. Think about what you're doing. You're pulling the rug away and letting them fall to the depths. Your child doesn't know why this is happening, and it's so fucking unfair. When he finally hits the bottom, he has to build some kind of foundation for himself, and that poor kid is scraping to find anything and climb on top of it and get that foundation to be himself. Now that's his journey, to learn about himself because of what happened. Think about that. Every dad should think about that before he makes a move in that direction.

Am I glad I *didn't* do some things? Yes. The one thing I'm glad I didn't do was take vengeance on the motherfucker who killed my brother. I can't emphasize that enough. I'm glad some kind of light came into my head when I was in that dark place, because it changed my path. That light was my upbringing, and my family telling me not to do it. I'd be dead, or in jail, and I wouldn't have my beautiful family, and I wouldn't be talking to you right now.

•••

THIS BOOK IS A message to you. Thank you for taking the time to read it—that means more to me than you'll ever know. If you're a father, or a son, or a brother, or anyone of any gender who loves their family, then I hope this book makes you a little bit stronger and more dedicated to looking after those great, unique people.

I also wrote this book for my loved ones, and especially for my son. It says, "This is what your dad did, and if I can help you in any way in life, this is how I can do it." I want the message to be: "It can be done. Here are the instructions. Use them for your own path." Whoever you are, you can do this. And my other message is that I'm still hungry. Whatever the next stage is, I want to get there and make the most of it. Never say die.

I know I'm fucked up from my childhood. My task in life is not to pass that on to my son, and to make his early life better for him than mine was for me. I know I overdo it, because I want to protect him from anything like that, but I want to make sure he's safe, and I want to make sure everything is done the right way for him.

There will be a time in my life when the option of walking on a stage isn't there anymore. I hope it's a long time from now because I can't imagine what it will be like not to have the thing that I treasure any more. I mean it—I treasure the time I have onstage, because I feel really lucky to have any of it. It's the ultimate drug that you can't get enough of. That's scary to think of. I want to enjoy each fucking moment. Grasp that moment!

That's what I do, because life is so short. Make sure you do it, too.

Frank Bello
New York City, 2021

Acknowledgments

MY LOVE AND GRATITUDE goes first and foremost to all the members of the Bello, Benante, Lobasso, Piacquadio, Salaman, and Tinnerello families.

I salute my current and former brothers in Anthrax: Joey Belladonna, Charlie Benante, John Bush, Rob Caggiano, Paul Crook, Jon Donais, Scott Ian, Danny Lilker, Dan Spitz, and Neil Turbin.

The band that got me started was Kiss. Thanks to Gene Simmons for his early inspiration and friendship, and for writing this book's foreword. Eternal respect to Paul Stanley, Ace Frehley, and Peter Criss.

To Rush, Cheap Trick, and Barbra Streisand for showing me the power of music.

Thanks to my colleagues in Metallica, Slayer, Megadeth, Overkill, Pantera, Iron Maiden, Public Enemy, Black Sabbath, and all the bands whom we've toured with over the years.

Respect to my bass heroes: Steve Harris, Geddy Lee, and Geezer Butler.

To friends and comrades: Armando Aguirre, Gene Ambo, Tom Browne, Andy Buchanan, Josh Bernstein, Missi Callazzo, Carl Canedy, Suzy Cole, Paul Collis, Melissa Cross, Jeff Cummings, Chuck D, Dom DeLuca, Tim Dralle, David Ellefson, Lady Gaga,

John Gallagher, Sharon Gilday, Corey Glover, Bill Gould, Page Hamilton, Rita Haney, Matt Hanrahan, Gary Holt, Mike Inez, Neil Ingleman, Chris Jericho, Robert John, Bill Kelliher, Kerry King, Janet Kleinbaum, Eddie Kramer, Chris LaRosa, Joe Marotta, John Mazzotta, Tim McGlinchey, Michael Mitnick, Saraphina Monaco, Mike and Jessica Monterulo, Jeff Moore, Mike Nicolari, Mark Pasche, Chuck Perry, Bill Philputt, Dug Pinnick, Mike Pucc, Norman Reedus, Art Ring, Jay Ruston, Adam Scott, Jeremy Skoorka, Brian Slagel, Lady Starlight, Corey Taylor, John Tempesta, Mike Tempesta, Zach Throne, Mike Toto, Eddie Trunk, Geri Upton, Joey and Tracy Vera, Mark Weiss, Zakk Wylde, and Neil Zlozower.

To the memory of those no longer with us: Darrell "Dimebag" Abbott, Vinnie Paul Abbott, Cliff Burton, Eric Carr, Ronnie James Dio, Lemmy Kilmister, Layne Staley, Jon Zazula, and Marsha Zazula.

Heartfelt thanks to my gear companies Charvel, D'Addario, EMG, ESP, Hartke, Monster Energy, and Monster Music.

I raise my glass to my acting coach Bill Esper, to my cowriter Joel McIver and my publisher Tyson Cornell, to Hailie, Alexandra, and Guy at Rare Bird Lit, and finally to all fans of Anthrax. I can't thank you enough. You're the best people in the world.

Index

All songs and albums by Anthrax except as noted. In the Bello and Benante entries, relationships to Frank are indicated.

Abbott, Darrell ("Dimebag") 15, 75, 128, 142, 143, 144, 145, 146, 160–161, 162, 199
Abbott, Vinnie Paul 142, 146, 161–162
Accept (band) 76
Actors Studio 123
Agent Steel 74, 75
Alda, Alan 185
Algrant, Dan 183
Alice In Chains 105, 116
Alive! (Kiss album) 31
Altitudes & Attitude 98, 191–192, 199
"Am I Evil?" (Diamond Head song) 179
Among The Living 78, 89, 90, 92, 162
"(Anesthesia) Pulling Teeth" (Metallica song) 58
Anthems 193
Anthrax Day (September 14) 180
Applegate, Christina 119
Araya, Tom 118
Armed and Dangerous 61, 62, 64
Armored Saint 125, 154, 160
Aucoin, Bill 34

Back to the Future (movie) 155
Bambi (movie) 185
Barrowland Ballroom (venue) 76
Beacon Theater (venue) 115
Beastie Boys 106, 112
Beatles 39
Belladonna, Joey 61, 62, 68, 77, 94, 98, 118, 126, 127, 162, 176, 177, 179, 180
Bello, Anthony (brother) 15, 16, 124, 125, 130, 131, 132, 133, 134, 135, 136, 137, 138–140, 141, 147, 150, 164, 165
Bello, Brandon (son) 14, 22, 96, 137, 150, 166, 168, 169, 170, 171, 172, 173, 174
Bello, Charles ("Chuck," brother) 15, 131, 134
Bello, Frank: born 15, parents 15, bullied at school 17–18, 21–22, moves to grandmother's house 19, love of food 20–21, 25, 74, 75, works at deli 22–24, drug experiences 28–29, paternal grandparents 29–30, plays guitar and bass 30, 46, love for old New York 40–42, on heavy metal 45–46, Anthrax roadie 48, joins Anthrax 50–52, first show 53–54, early tours 54–56, relationships 66, dealing with fame 68, on bass playing 89–90, music as therapy 95–97, tour pranks 103–104, debauchery 104–105, on touring economics 107–109, fighting 110, on Chuck D 114–116, on acting 121–124, the 'Kirk's door' incident 128–130, the death of Anthony and aftermath 130–140, marries Teresa 147–148, plays with Helmet 157–161, rejoins Anthrax 162, becomes a father 166–168, on fatherhood 169–174, 203, on stagecraft and film/TV 183–190, auditions 188–190, the future 201, 204
Bello, Rose (mother) 15, 16, 17, 19, 20, 25–26, 43, 50, 56, 57, 69, 95, 132, 134, 136, 169
Bello, Suzanne (sister) 15, 134
Bello, Teresa (wife) 13, 20, 43, 82, 98, 111, 112, 115, 116, 135, 136, 141, 147, 148, 149, 166, 167, 168, 169, 170, 172, 173, 174
Bello, Tonianne (sister) 15, 134
Benante, Angela (aunt) 19
Benante, Bernadette ("Tina," grandmother) 19, 20, 21, 25, 47–48, 50, 69, 89, 92, 95, 97–98, 99, 136, 180–181, 202
Benante, Charles (grandfather) 19
Benante, Charlie (uncle) 19, 30, 31, 32, 33, 44, 46, 47, 48, 50, 51, 56, 59, 60, 64, 67, 80, 81, 86, 90, 92–93, 95, 98, 99, 106, 107, 112, 115, 127, 128, 132, 137, 138, 148, 150, 155, 157, 162, 163, 175, 180, 181
Benante, Laurie (aunt) 19, 20, 22, 50, 134, 169
Benante, Mia (cousin) 81, 167
Benante, Susan (aunt) 19, 20, 22, 23
"Big Four" Sonisphere dates 177–181, 191

Bill & Ted's Bogus Journey (movie) 187
Billy, Chuck 193
"Black Diamond" (Kiss song), 33
Black Sabbath 72, 179
Black Tooth Grin (cocktail) 142, 143, 162
Blackwell, Chris 78
Bon Jovi (band) 93
Bono (Paul Hewson, U2) 80
"Booze and Cigarettes" (Altitudes & Attitude song) 98
"Born Again Idiot" 160
"Bring the Noise" (Public Enemy song) 112, 113
Brown, Rex 198, 199
Browne, Tom 32, 34, 35, 36, 37, 38, 39, 50
Buchanan, Andy 76
Buckley, Jeff 182
Buckley, Tim 182
Burton, Cliff 57–58, 84–85, 86, 88, 89, 92
Bush, John 61, 85, 125, 126, 154, 176
Butler, Geezer 55, 62, 91

Caddyshack (movie) 184
"Cadillac Rock Box" 160
Caggiano, Rob 98, 151, 192–193
Callazzo, Missi 119
Canedy, Carl 61, 62, 63–64, 65
Cantorial (play) 188
Cantrell, Jerry 116–117
Carr, Eric 38
"Caught in a Mosh" 79–80, 107
CBGB (club) 49
Cheap Trick 43–44, 91, 104
Checker, Chubby 31
Cher 67
Chernobyl disaster 74
Chuck D (Carlton Ridenhour, Public Enemy) 114, 115, 116
Cinderella (band) 93
Clash of the Titans (tour) 116, 117
Clayton, Adam 80
Crazy Nights (Kiss album) 39
Creatures of the Night (Kiss album) 36
Criss, Peter 32–33
Crook, Paul 131, 132, 138, 150

Death Angel 193, 197
"Deathrider" 54
Dee, Mikkey 155
Denim and Leather (Saxon album) 45

De Niro, Robert 42, 183
"Detroit Rock City" (Kiss song), 33
Dickinson, Bruce 195
Dimebag – see Abbott, Darrell
Dio, Ronnie James 72, 91, 94–95, 179
Dio (band) 93
Dodson, Mark 106–107
Donais, Jon 193
Download festival 165

Eastwood, Clint 121
Edge, The (Dave Evans, U2) 80
Eilish, Billie 171
Electric Lady Studios 44
Elektra (label) 58, 126, 127, 146
Ellefson, David 98, 191
Esper, Bill 121, 123, 124
"Evergreen" (Barbra Streisand song) 43
Exodus (band) 105, 193

Faith No More 199, 200
Fallon, Matt 61
Fistful of Metal 23, 49, 52
Flav, Flavor (William Drayton Jr., Public Enemy) 114, 115
For All Kings 194–195
Fox, Michael J. 155
Freeman, Morgan 121
Frehley, Ace 32, 33

Gallagher, John 55
Gervais, Ricky 70
Get It Out (Altitudes & Attitude album) 199
Giants Stadium 80
Gigantour 165
Glover, Corey 104
Goodfellas (movie) 111
"Got the Time" (Joe Jackson song) 106–107
Gould, Bill 200
Grammy awards 70, 80
Greetings from Tim Buckley (movie) 181, 186–187
"Gung-Ho" 64

Hagar, Sammy 32
Hamilton, Page 158, 159, 161
Hammersmith Odeon (venue) 95
Hammett, Kirk 85, 86, 127, 128, 129, 130, 178
Harris, Steve 44–45, 55, 62, 63, 68, 71, 91, 156, 192, 195, 196–197

FRANK BELLO

Hartke (amps) 191, 192
Headbangers Ball Tour 105
"Heaven and Hell" (Black Sabbath song) 91, 179
Heaven and Hell (Black Sabbath album) 91
Heaven and Hell (band) 94
Hell, Richard 181, 182, 183–184
Helloween 105
Helmet (band) 158, 159, 160, 161, 162, 163, 164
Hetfield, James 85, 86, 87, 127, 128, 178, 179–180
Hughes, Mick ("Big Mick") 88
Hughes, Glenn 72
Hyatt House (hotel) 105

"I Am the Law" 92
Ian, Scott 47, 48, 49, 51, 57, 61, 64, 67, 77, 90, 92, 98, 104, 106, 107, 109, 112, 127, 128, 137, 150, 153, 157, 162, 163, 175, 202
Ignition Records 146
"I'm the Man" 92, 126
Inez, Mike 105
"Inside Out" 160
Iommi, Tony 72
Iron Maiden 44, 51, 75, 78, 79, 109, 156, 188, 195–196, 197
Irvine Meadows Amphitheatre 109
Island Records 66, 67–68, 69, 71, 78

Jackson, Joe 106
Joe's Apartment (movie) 188
Joe's Deli 22, 23, 24, 27, 28, 56, 61, 69, 70, 73, 78, 89, 92
Judas Priest 47, 151
Judge Dredd 92

Kelliher, Bill 199
Kenny, Michael 156
Killswitch Engage 194
King, Kerry 118
"King Size" 160
Kings X 104
Kiss (band) 31, 32–33, 34–35, 36, 37, 38, 39, 43, 51, 79
Kleinbaum, Janet 67
Klugman, Jack 185
Knebworth House (venue) 180
Knight, Ted 184
Korn 150

Kramer, Eddie 79, 90

Lady Gaga 81
Lamb of God (band) 194
L'Amour (club) 53, 75, 76, 78
Law and Order (TV) 156–157
Led Zeppelin 39, 79, 105
Lee, Geddy 30, 55, 62, 63, 91
Lemmon, Jack 185
Lemmy (Ian Kilmister) 85, 101, 154–155
Lick It Up (Kiss album) 36
Lilker, Danny 47, 48, 50, 51, 67
Limp Bizkit 150
Little Kids Rock 192
Living Colour 104
Lombardo, Dave 118
"Lone Justice" 63
Looney Tunes (TV) 185
Love Gun (Kiss album) 32
Lyxzén, Dennis 199–200

Maby, Graham 106
MacLeod, Gavin 184
"Madhouse" 68
Marley, Bob 67
Married...with Children (TV) 118–120, 121, 183
M*A*S*H* (TV) 184–185
Mastodon (band)
Matthau, Walter 185
McBrain, Nicko 196–197
McCartney, Paul 80–81,90
McIver, Joel 14, 17
Megacruise 199
Megadeth 98, 116, 117, 177, 178, 191
Megaforce (label) 66, 119
Meisner Technique 123
Metal Allegiance (band) 118
Metal Alliance (tour) 193
Metallica 57, 58, 75, 78, 83, 84, 85, 86, 87, 88, 92, 93, 127, 129, 130, 177, 178
Method acting 123
Milano, Billy 67
Minto, Zeb 196
Mitnick, Michael 101–102
Monsters of Rock (festival) 92, 93
Monterulo, Mike 98, 137, 162
Motörhead 44, 85, 154
Moving Pictures (Rush album) 28, 30–31
Mullen, Larry Jr. 80
Mustaine, Dave 180

"Neon Knights" (Black Sabbath song) 91
Netflix 80
Newsted, Jason 92
New York Music Awards 115
New York Steel (concert) 153
New York Times 47
Nuclear Blast (label) 151
Nu-metal 151, 154

Oidivnikufesin (video) 95
O'Neill, Ed 119, 120–121
"Only" 85
"Open Letter (To a Landlord)" (Living Colour song) 104
Osbourne, Ozzy 72, 91, 105
Osegueda, Mark 193
Overkill (band) 74, 75
Owens, Tim ('Ripper') 151

Pantera 141, 142, 143, 144, 145, 146, 198
"Penny Lane" (Beatles song) 90
Persistence of Time 93, 106, 108, 119, 126
Petersson, Tom 91, 104
Piacquadio, Joe 22, 23, 23, 27, 69, 78, 89
Piece of Mind (Iron Maiden album) 44
"Pieces" 137, 138–140
Pinnick, Dug 104
Playboy (magazine) 30
Police, The 81, 82
Public Enemy 112, 113, 114, 115, 116, 117, 126

Radiohead 193
Randall, Tony 185
Raven (band) 55, 57
Records & Stuff (store) 28
Reedus, Norman 197–198
Refused (band) 200
Richards, Keith 67
Rickles, Don 82, 83
"Riding Shotgun" 160
Right Track Studios 36
Rock Star (movie) 105
Rods (band) 62
Rolling Stones 79
Roseland Ballroom 57, 58
Rush 28, 30, 31, 42, 44, 51, 91
Ruston, Jay 191

Sadler, William 186
Saturday Night Fever (movie) 27

Saxon (band) 45
"Schism" 100
Scorsese, Martin 25, 28, 40, 42, 70, 111, 133
Shadows Fall 193
Simmons, Gene 13, 16, 32, 33, 35, 36, 37, 38, 39, 45, 61, 71, 107, 190, 197, 201
Singer, Eric 72
Size Matters (Helmet album) 159
Skolnick, Alex 193
Slayer 116, 117, 118, 177, 178, 181, 197, 198
Slipknot 175
SnoCore tour 159
S.O.D.—see Stormtroopers of Death
"Somewhere" (Barbra Streisand song) 43
Sonisphere festival 176
Sound of White Noise 93, 126
Soundwave festival 176
South By Southwest festival 159
South Park (TV) 185
Speak English or Die (Stormtroopers of Death album) 67
Spitz, Danny 51, 72, 162
Spitz, Dave 72
Spreading the Disease 62–64, 67, 68, 90, 92
Springsteen, Bruce 80
Staley, Layne 116
Stanley, Paul 32, 33, 35, 61
State of Euphoria 93, 100
Sting (Gordon Sumner) 81–82, 156
Stomp 442 127, 146, 160
Stormtroopers of Death 67, 150
Stranger Things (TV) 33, 35, 39
"Strap it On" 160
Strasberg, Lee 123
Streets (nightclub) 111
Streisand, Barbra 43, 46

Taylor, Corey 175, 176
Tchaikovsky, Pyotr 46
Tempesta, John 47, 158, 159, 161
Tempesta, Mike 47, 51
Terminator X (Norman Rogers, Public Enemy) 114
Testament (band) 92, 193
"The Bends" (Radiohead song) 193
The Bugs Bunny Show (TV) 185
The Godfather (movie) 186
The Greater of Two Evils 156
The Irishman (movie) 42
The Love Boat (TV) 184

The Mary Tyler Moore Show (TV) 184, 185
The Odd Couple (movie/TV) 158, 185
The Shawshank Redemption (movie) 187
The Simpsons (TV) 185
The Sopranos (TV) 188
The Tonight Show Starring Johnny Carson (TV) 82
"The Twist" (Chubby Checker song) 31
The Walking Dead (TV) 197
Traynor, Chris 159
Trespass (movie) 187
Trunk, Eddie 153
Turbin, Neil 51, 52, 59
Twisted Sister 153
Tyler Moore, Mary 184

U2 67, 80
Ulrich, Lars 85, 86, 127, 128, 129
Uncle Joe– see Piacquadio, Joe
Ungar, Felix 158
US Speed Metal Tour 72

Van Halen (band) 142, 144, 145
Van Halen, Eddie 142
Vera, Joey 160
Volbeat 192
Volume 8: The Threat Is Real 137, 146, 160

W.A.S.P. (band) 93
"We Care a Lot" (Faith No More song) 199
We've Come For You All 154, 156, 160
World Trade Center attacks, 2001 ("9/11") 151–153
Worship Music 180, 194
Wylde, Zakk 105

Yankee Stadium 180
"Young and Wasted" (Kiss song) 38
"YYZ" (Rush song) 91

Zander, Robin 44
Zazula, John 56, 66, 83
Zazula, Marsha 56